Project Management for the Pharmaceutical Industry

Project Management for the Pharmaceutical Industry

LAURA BROWN
and
TONY GRUNDY

Routledge
Taylor & Francis Group

LONDON AND NEW YORK

First published 2011 by Gower Publishing

2 Park Square, Milton Park, Abingdon, Oxon OX14 4RN
711 Third Avenue, New York, NY 10017, USA

Routledge is an imprint of the Taylor & Francis Group, an informa business

First issued in paperback 2016

British Library Cataloguing in Publication Data
Brown, Laura (Laura Sophia Rose)
    Project management for the pharmaceutical industry. – Rev. ed.
    1. Project management. 2. Pharmaceutical industry – Management.
    I. Title II. Grundy, Tony, 1954–
    615.1'0684–dc22

ISBN 978-1-4094-1894-8 (hbk)
ISBN 978-1-138-24742-0 (pbk)

Library of Congress Control Number: 2010939802

Contents

List of Figures

List of Tables

Preface

Project management has been a well embedded technique outside the pharmaceutical sector for many decades now. But in the last decade it has become increasingly important within the pharma industry.

This industry is one which traditionally had been previously relatively insulated from intense competitive pressure, and is thus a latecomer to full-blown project management. But now due to over the increasing threat of generic drugs, increasing regulatory requirements, health innovations and the wave of mergers in the mid/late 1990s and early 2000s it is no longer possible to manage the business without it – and it must also be taken beyond its simplest and most mechanistic form.

Since the first edition of this book was published these pressures have significantly intensified with the disruptive effects of the credit crunch, recession and soaring public sector deficits and government borrowing worldwide. This is leading governments to seek better value for money out of big pharma. In parallel, as global demand for drugs increases, as result of an increasingly ageing population and through medical advances, the viability of finances of health services across the world will be threatened.

In addition, in the US, President Obama has wasted no time in addressing the regulatory and economic provisions for drug development, purchasing and pricing – these changes will put more pressure indirectly on the management of pharma projects. Concerns too about the dangers attendant to side effects from drugs will make it much more risky to roll out any blockbuster drugs – so the more likely scenario in future will be that such drugs will be gradually exploited over a range of therapeutic applications. This will greatly dilute the economic benefit of the blockbuster effect through slowing down value creation, and through increasing the costs and complexity of drug development. The whole area of risk management will become far more important even than before.

Also there are a significant number of drugs coming off-patent resulting in many companies having limited pipelines. Pharma projects therefore need to be managed more strategically as companies will have a squeeze on the resource they can plough back into R&D due to pressures on average margins – and even more pressure will be placed on completing projects within timelines as well as to control, if not to reduce, cost.

President Obama also wants into encourage the expansion of the generics market – making further inroads into the traditional terrain of big pharma. In sum, pharma companies will have to do a lot more – and with less – and even then returns are unlikely to be as great. This suggests that project management processes will have to be ever sharper for companies to succeed.

Increases in competitive change led to intensified internal pressure to deliver much faster – and to reduce time to market. The pharma industry increasingly has looked to project management to accelerate drug development and particularly the clinical research part of the process. Unfortunately the industry has tended to see projects as standardised, and as relatively uniform, which in reality they were not. As one of the authors, Laura Brown, reflects:

> *Each clinical trial project is different from the rest. You may have a different population to trial the drug out on, a drug with different beneficial effects and method of administration, and a different project team. There may also be a different set of regulatory stakeholders to manage. Above all, the organisational timing and context will be unique. As a result, a project team, relying primarily on activity analysis and computer software, critical path and resource planning, will still tend to get bogged down in internal politics, will struggle with often inadequate resources, inadequate project training and project team development. And this is before having to deal with endemic difficulties of recruiting patients on a just-in-time basis – and likewise clearing regulatory hurdles.*

This example demonstrates that even within a more *technical* project environment we see projects as beset with environmental uncertainty, with interdependencies, and with struggles to allocate strategically, and all within a complex organisational environment.

The Pharmaceutical Project Management Process

Traditional project management is therefore not up to the challenge posed by the pharma industry and needs to be augmented by other perspectives. These perspectives include the strategic, operational, organisational and also the financial, as we see in Figure P.1.

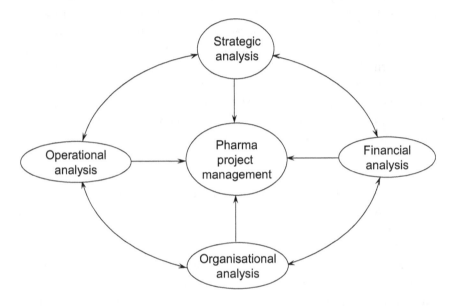

Figure P.1   Perspectives on pharmaceutical project management

The authors' own process developed over many years as a response to the increasing number and diversity of business projects which we and managers were facing in the pharma industry. Initially we began by looking at how managers could link business projects back to the strategic goals of their business. Drawing on the PhD research of one of the authors (into strategic and financial project appraisal) we were then able to bring in techniques of assessing how pharma projects add to, dilute or even destroy shareholder value. This helped to integrate project management with both strategic and financial analysis, which are often not well linked in the pharma industry.

Next, we brought in approaches to assessing implementation difficulty drawn originally from organisational theory – particularly in applying force-field analysis. (Around ten years ago the project management literature generally was almost totally devoid of any mention of force-field analysis.) This approach was then further enriched by bringing in stakeholder analysis techniques (which are particularly important for pharma projects, given their technical and political complexity), and was found in the strategy literature, and now developed further in this book.

Operational analysis was also helpful in extending and enriching traditional project management – as practised in the pharma industry. For instance, as managers appeared to lack adequate problem-solving in the definition of many projects, we were drawn to the diagnosis technique of fishbone analysis which is normally associated with Total Quality Management (TQM). Moving on, then, to the imperative to prioritise projects more effectively, we brought in Attractiveness–Implementation Difficulty (AID) analysis, which had been discovered in managing cost breakthroughs when working with the pharma company, then called Amersham-Nycomed, some years ago.

Project uncertainty was clearly one of the main reasons why traditional project management techniques ended up producing spuriously accurate but unrealistic project plans in the pharma industry. This led us to look at what help strategic management could provide, and to scenario analysis in particular. We incorporated the uncertainty grid to help surface and evaluate key project assumptions for pharma projects along with traditional risk assessment techniques already well known in the pharma industry. Later on this was expanded to incorporate scenario-generating and story-telling techniques to help flesh-out and explore the possible trajectories which each pharma project might take.

Finally, in the late 1990s, one of us undertook some fascinating research into senior managers' behaviour when engaged in managing major projects (Grundy, 1998b). This study focused on a small but influential team of technical strategists who were engaged in project managing some major breakthroughs in the organisation. Besides discovering much about how and why teams tend to get so entangled in seeking to manage complex projects, some very practical techniques for monitoring and managing both the dynamics of projects were drawn out, and of the somewhat turbulent behaviours associated with them. (We will see these later in Chapter 7, 'Influencing People and Behaviour', how to cope with these more effectively.)

So, our approach to *Project Management for the Pharmaceutical Industry* is very much an eclectic one, which manages projects as part of overall programmes.

These 'programmes' help to implement business strategy and organisational breakthroughs of pharma companies.

Many pharma companies have now benefited from some or all of the techniques contained in this book. These include Altana, Amgen, Arrow Therapeutics, Tripos Receptor Research, Lilly, Novi Nordisk, Napp, Galderma and UCB. Hopefully, over time, these techniques will be taken up by your own company.

Our book will help a number of groups of manager, particularly:

- senior pharma managers engaged in turning business strategies into implementation through project management;

- practising middle and senior managers in pharma companies working on internal, cross-functional or within functional projects at a strategic level;

- pharmceutical professionals managing projects within their own roles.

Since this book was first published many pharma organisations and individual professionals have been using not merely the more traditional elements like critical path analysis and Gantt charts but also tools such as:

- strategic gap analysis;

- the project option grid;

- stakeholder analysis;

- force-field analysis;

- interdependency analysis;

for diagnosis, project strategy development, detailed planning, influencing and monitoring implementation. These highly visual tools have had a big impact on the clarity and transparency of complex project management processes.

Taking two quick examples of this:

- At one pharma company, the Clinical Research function used stakeholder analysis to influence and manage US stakeholders proactively to return project leadership to Europe, rather than managing this, with difficulty, from the US.

- At another very large European pharma company, the head of global training used the project option grid to evaluate options and to then prioritise plans for a Global Training Strategy.

Structure and Content of this Book

Project Management for the Pharmaceutical Industry is structured as follows:

- Chapter 1 looks at how pharma projects need to be managed strategically.

- Chapter 2 turns to the key links of pharma projects with pharma business strategy.

- Chapter 3 looks at the pharma project process itself, considering the first two phases of pharma project definition (and diagnosis).

- Chapter 4 examines phases II and III of the project management process by considering Project Strategy and Plans together and contains the core of the project management tools – both traditional and new.

- Chapter 5 explores the intricacies of project evaluation and, in particular, how we can grapple with the difficulties of putting a realistic financial value on a pharma project. (Many project management books either refer to texts on Financial Project Appraisal or tend to regard this area as a question purely of Discounted Cash Flow (DCF). We take the view that prior to the deployment of DCF techniques we also need to perform analysis of key value and cost drivers impacting on pharma projects, and (potentially) to describe some key project scenarios.)

- Chapter 6 we focuses on the practicalities of making projects happen, including project mobilisation. This chapter contains a number of formats for detailed project management systems and controls. We also take a brief look at how information technology (IT) systems have changed project management processes.

- Chapter 7 examines the more purely people and behavioural dimensions of project management – not only through project management systems, but also through documentation processes and the Internet.

- Chapter 8 looks at a number of generic types of projects and explores some tailored checklists for applying project management to them. These include:

  - R&D projects;
  - acquisition projects;
  - alliance and joint venture projects;
  - operational improvement projects; and
  - organisational change projects.

- Chapter 9 shows how these techniques can be deployed both to micro-issues within your own role. This chapter also finally draws together the key lessons on project management and focuses especially on how to implement the techniques.

Throughout the book you are invited to invest some time in working through exercises on your own projects so that you can extract maximum learning. Whilst some readers may be tempted to skim these they *really will* enhance your retention and incorporation of the tools and techniques by the order of at least 100 per cent. *Please do not be tempted just to browse the book.*

In conclusion, *Project Management for the Pharmaceutical Industry* has developed from many sources. All of these sources are essential in order to get real value out of these projects, not to mention making your life in pharma companies generally less stressful! We now urge you therefore to read, digest and to apply this book which we have been most fortunate to have project managed.

Managing Pharmaceutical Projects Strategically

Introduction

In this chapter we first take a further look at the deficiencies of conventional project management in relation to the pharma industry. Then we explore the need for strategic thinking in managing projects. We illustrate this with a case study drawn from one of the author's experiences of project managing pharma projects at a biosciences division of ICI (now AstraZeneca). Finally, we introduce the five key steps of the pharma project management process:

- defining the project;

- creating the project strategy;

- detailed project planning;

- implementation and control;and

- review and learning.

Throughout the book you will be invited to invest some time in working through exercises on your own projects so that you can extract maximum learning. Whilst some readers may be tempted to skim these they *really will* enhance your retention and incorporation of the tools and techniques by the order of at least 100 per cent. *Please do not be tempted just to browse the book.*

Deficiencies in Conventional Project Management

Conventional project management is very much the offspring of Taylorian Scientific Management. Although the idea that management is a science, and should be managed as such, is no longer much in vogue, the rationalist assumptions embedded in project management carry on.

Not that there is anything in principle wrong with the idea that business projects can and should be managed on a rational basis. Indeed this book very much springs from that premise, however much modified its approach – to deal with the messier aspects of projects. Nevertheless, we believe it is important to avoid the naivety of assuming that rational analysis is the prime mover in project management. Chapter 7, in particular, highlights the role of people and behaviour in the project management process. This is especially relevant in any R&D context – as managers are likely to be emotionally and politically attached to certain technical approaches to project implementation. Rather than being a little extra, an add-on to the more rational techniques of project management, the softer, behaviour-related aspects are fundamental in this industry.

Whilst many generic books on project management contain something on the behavioural side, one's impression is that this is very much about 'by the way, whilst you are at it, remember that people need to be managed alongside the projects'. For the very heart of conventional project management texts centres, invariably, on activity management – the targeting, scheduling, measuring and controlling of tangible activities through time.

The real issue is not just about the management of project detail. It is also about making sure that managers do not lose sight of the really big picture. 'Why are managers even doing this project and not another one?' is often a very real question to ask, even if this seems unthinkable at times in the pharma industry, and even if the project is a given, we have found in the pharma context there are still – invariably – many different ways of implementing them.

Also, where pharma projects are inherently uncertain, the relatively precise definition of activity durations can become almost an academic irrelevancy. Further, as pharma projects are particularly vulnerable to knock-on effects, the most important critical success factor seems to be to identify how these projects can be *made more resilient generally* rather than worrying about whether a particular activity might overrun by 10 per cent or so.

Now please try the following exercise which is designed to tease out the importance of a pharma project's strategic context:

EXERCISE – REVIEWING THE PROJECT'S OBJECTIVES

For one pharma project which you have undertaken in the past:

- Why did you embark on this project?
- If you cannot easily say why, what *should* have been your objectives (looking back)?
- Where the project ran into difficulties, to what extent were these due to:
  - traditional deficiencies in project management (for example, estimating the time, resource management and monitoring);
  - less tangible deficiencies (for example, politics, stakeholder agendas, ownership of goals, interdependencies, uncertainties, and so on)?

The above exercise is likely to have shown that you may not have had sufficient process in your project. But you can have too much process, rather than too little.

Project management ought not to imply a burdensome bureaucracy. Indeed, in today's pharma industry the organisational imperatives can kill organisational speed by placing extensive form-filling demands on you for all projects.

Further, the advent of personal computers may not necessarily have helped either. Whilst fulfilling a useful role in helping project managers capture key data for projects, there may be a tendency to collect information so that it can just go on the computer. (In fact we have heard a number of project management practitioners say that the *last* thing one should do is to put project details onto project management software. In their view it is essential to make sure that a company has got used to project management routines first.)

So looking back at your exercise (above) were not the most difficult issues of your project of a less tangible nature?

We are not, of course, suggesting for a moment that one should not perform activity analyses, and in considerable detail. We are merely highlighting that it is essential to keep a very strong sense of proportion when doing so, and especially to avoid making it look more complicated than it is. If one does over-complicate things, then one will surely miss the other and frequently more crucial issues which surround *why* we are doing the pharma project, *what value* do we hope to get out of it, and how can we avoid the greatest sources of difficulty.

So let us now begin to draw the contrast between the traditional and a more contemporary form of project management, which we advocate, and which is more relevant to the diversity and complexity of projects found in the pharma industry.

Table 1.1   Traditional versus contemporary project management

	Traditional project management	**Contemporary project management**
Link(s) with business strategy	Vague and distant	Direct and explicit
Project definition	Usually portrayed as a 'given'	Highly flexible, creative, and depending on options
Project planning	Follows on directly from project definition	Only done once a programme and its interdependencies are set
Attitude to detail	Absolutely central – it is all about control	Important but only in context – try always to see the 'big ("helicopter") picture' – around the project
The importance of stakeholders	Emphasis on formal structures – project manager, team sponsor	Far-reaching stakeholder analysis; requires continual scanning
The importance of uncertainty	Coped with through critical path analysis (after activity planning)	Perform uncertainty analysis first, then plan activities

You are now invited to reflect on the critical success factors of a post-pharma project.

EXERCISE – REFLECTING ON A PAST PHARMA PROJECT

Thinking back to a project in which you have been involved in the past, to what extent should its critical success factors be addressed by:

- Traditional project management approaches?
- More contemporary project management approaches?

and to what extent were these addressed for this project?

The Relevance of Strategic Thinking to Pharmaceutical Project Management

Strategic thinking is an essential part of managing projects in the pharma industry. First of all, business projects do often materialise as a result of formal strategy development. For instance, in the ICI Biosciences case study described later in this chapter, the ambitious growth plans ICI (now AstraZeneca) had for a biotech division involved a number of acquisitions, which were projects, and these led to an even greater number of integration projects. In addition to projects which are external-facing, there are frequently internal projects which are aimed at achieving major organisational change, for example, SmithKline Beecham's (now GSK) 'Simply-Better-Way' project, for change within the organisation.

Secondly, strategy comes in at the level of the individual pharma project which has materialised in relative isolated basis. Each project of that kind then needs to be linked back up to the business strategy of the pharma company. This should be accomplished by teasing out the strategic objectives of each and every major pharma project.

A third level for strategy input is within the pharma project itself, for each and every project has both an internal environment and, hopefully, also some strategy for achieving its own, inherent advantage.

Strategic thinking is often associated with 'very big picture' thinking. But, in reality, there is just the same need for more localised strategic thinking for specific pharma projects as there is at that much higher level. Also, as we have already mentioned, the more narrow, operational focus of projects does tend to lead people to ask the question, 'Why do I need a strategy for that pharma project?'

So what does 'strategic thinking' mean more generally? It can be defined as:

> *The creative and relentless pursuit of options for action which leverage resources, and produce shareholder value more easily and in less time.*

Strategic thinking thus contains a number of key elements:

- Creative: strategic thinking requires thinking outside the box.

- Relentless: it is not something just purely intuitive, but typically requires analysis techniques.

- Options: invariably there are many options, not merely for *what* you could do, but also for *how* you might do it.

- Action: strategic thinking does mean thinking in concrete terms of the actions that will be needed – by whom and by when.

- Leverage: strategic thinking is continually focused on getting a lot out of the minimum.

- Shareholder value: the generation of cash flows which profile over time is more than enough to cover the cost of capital.

Strategic thinking is often depicted as 'helicopter thinking'. This is now embedded in the strategic thinking guides of diverse pharma companies (see Figure 1.1) including Amgen, Amersham plc, Tripos Receptor Research, and others.

Figure 1.1 depicts a helicopter flying over rough, hostile terrain. The alternative to the helicopter (walking) only obscures vision – notice how the competitor with the bow and arrow is concealed from vision – and the project's customer, whether external or internal. Also, there is every tendency (if walking) to go down the rabbit holes – which are inordinately interesting.

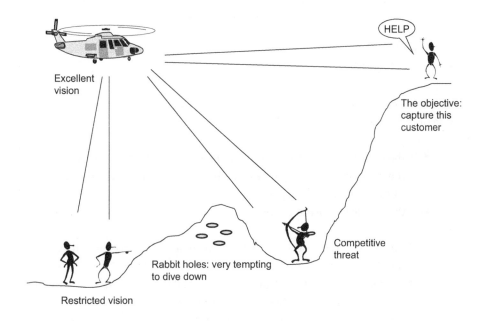

Excellent vision

HELP

The objective: capture this customer

Rabbit holes: very tempting to dive down

Competitive threat

Restricted vision

Figure 1.1   Helicopter vision

Having made extensive use of this picture over the past eight years we coined the phrase 'rabbit-hole management' to capture the fact that going down the rabbit holes can become *too much* of a habit (this is especially relevant for pharma projects which often involve a lot of complex, technical detail). Figure 1.1 should be used during each and every major project management meeting in order to avoid too much preoccupation with the wrong level of detail. It is particularly useful for helping managers to avoid getting entangled in petty or narrow, personal agendas.

In summary, strategic (or 'helicopter') thinking is useful for:

- checking whether a particular pharma project is the appropriate vehicle for the strategy in any event;

- generating other options for implementing the pharma project;

- understanding key opportunities and threats that the project faces in its environment and its internal strengths and weaknesses;

- interrelating the project with others in order to understand its total rationale, and its value.

CASE EXAMPLE – MANAGING PROJECTS STRATEGICALLY: ICI BIOSCIENCES

We now examine a live illustration of project management in action as told by one of the authors. This case study highlights:

- the importance of prioritisation in pharma project management;
- the need to manage uncertainty, ambiguity and interdependencies;
- the importance of thorough diagnosis;
- the significance of the 'softer' factors, including stakeholder management.

Although the events of this story occurred some years ago, the experiences are as vivid as if they had happened yesterday. So let us time-travel back to when one of the authors was seconded from a large consulting group to become Head of Finance, Planning and Acquisitions for a division of ICI (now AstraZeneca). This business no longer operates in the same or even similar form to the way it did then. We will call the division 'ICI Biosciences'. This case study illustrates a range of projects which posed major management difficulties.

ICI Biosciences was a (then) £100 million turnover mini-group of companies with operations in three countries:

- UK: a major research centre; also some minor manufacturing activities.
- US: a significant biosciences business with manufacturing facilities.
- Continental Europe: a very recently acquired business in continental Europe which was a major and successful manufacturing operation. (By 'recently' I mean one week before I arrived on the scene.)

ICI Biosciences' headquarters was located in a beautiful rural setting, in woodland. It shared a common site with a large part of the company which we will call ICI Global Technology. I was to have a joint reporting relationship to the European General Manager (who in turn reported to the Managing Director of the International Biosciences Division) and also to the Divisional Financial Controller, ICI Global Technology.

Following ICI's recent acquisition of its European manufacturing operation and the appointment of the former Head of Finance Planning and Acquisitions as its Finance Director, I was identified by my consulting company as being the 'ideal candidate' to be seconded for 'between three to six months' to fill this role.

Meanwhile, I had made the mistake of taking a *whole* two weeks' holiday in North Yorkshire. While I was combating the coastal sea mist (at the same time as the rest of the country was baking in 30°C heat), my superiors were busy plotting my next six months' work.

I returned to my desk on Monday morning expecting to have a week on low power. Instead, I found at note which read:

> *Dear Tony*
>
> *I expect you have had a most restful two weeks. I know how pleased you will be that we have found another project to keep you out of the office. From 9 am tomorrow you will be (until further notice) the Head of Finance, Planning and Acquisitions for the fast-growing, £100m turnover, ICI Biosciences.*
>
> *We know a bit about the assignment, which I can share with you. However, their finance people have offered to tell you more about it so I guess a quick session with myself and the client partner will help you gain a good overview.*
>
> *Oh, you may need to pack, as it is over 100 miles from Cambridge. I am sure you will be able to negotiate adequate living costs from your new client.*
>
> *Best of luck, your Consulting Partner, Ivan Moneybags*

This perhaps highlights our number one learning lesson in project management: unless you attempt to get someone's ownership of the project that they are being asked to manage, it might just undermine their commitment!

Looking back, it looks less than accidental that I was given so little thinking time to assimilate my latest 'mission'. Senior people, I suspect, often relish the task of choosing someone for a project – without any prior consent on their part. It is part of the inevitable power-play of organisations, but can be highly undermining to eventual delivery; managing difficult pharma business projects successfully requires a tremendous tenacity and single-mindedness that does not mix well with any sense of being made a victim.

But, returning to the ICI story, following the major acquisition in Europe this obviously raised integration issues which need to be project managed. Worse, the US subsidiary had posted some disappointing (to put it kindly) results. So this was a very urgent and important diagnosis project to ascertain why this had happened, what measures could be taken to ameliorate this situation, and to find out what lessons could be learned generally. Besides this, there were a number of R&D projects which required urgent financial appraisal.

Another (certain-to-become) project was the need to deliver a three-year divisional plan over the following three and a half months. This project would naturally be influenced by the outcome of integration work on both the US and (more recent) European acquisition.

In case anyone believes that I was about to have a really quiet time – away from the turmoil of consulting projects, then can I just add that the division was also contemplating another major acquisition in the UK. For the past decade acquisitions have been major projects in the pharma industry, presenting their own specific difficulties. Fortunately, ICI's bid was 'unsuccessful', which meant that I was not engulfed in post-integration work from that particular direction (the good news). The bad news was that no soon had we dried the tears from our eyes, immediately one manager spotted a smaller UK acquisition and another manager identified an additional acquisition target in Scandinavia.

'Absolutely great,' I thought when I heard the news.

With new projects coming thick and fast I was beginning to wonder whether I would ever escape even when my successor, a senior finance manager from elsewhere in the group, was due to arrive in four to six months' time.

My own team of three qualified accountants were also in something of a state on my arrival. Not only had two of them been working around the clock on the abortive UK acquisition immediately before my arrival, but their morale seemed at an all-time low. This acquisition had generated some interesting differences of opinion which had left them feeling somewhat bruised. And now they had some smart management consultant telling them what to do!

So, by this stage, if you have not felt project overload then you should have. Not only was there a potentially much greater project workload than could possibly be handled with the existing resource, but it threatened to get even worse. What other emergent projects could come out of the woodwork? Fortunately, I had already had my holiday so at least I did not have to project manage having that too.

Now it is apparent from this situation that:

- I faced a large number of projects;
- that most of these were ill-defined in terms of timescales, outputs, inputs, value and difficulty;
- there were significant interdependencies between these projects;
- the existing workload could be magnified by additional, emergent projects including further acquisitions, post-acquisition work, other business development projects, and also in setting up the necessary infrastructure to cope more effectively with high growth.

On top of these projects I had three additional projects to manage:

1. I had been thinking about moving consulting firms for some time and the letter I had on my desk on my return from Yorkshire was the limit of what I was prepared to tolerate. I needed, in the same period of time, to find a job in another consulting firm and to achieve this *without detriment to the ICI Biosciences secondment* (which might otherwise have tarnished my reputation, which I sought to retain intact).
2. As the secondment ran through the summer months, I wanted to move my family down to ICI (from 120 miles away) so that they were not bored silly over the summer months – and I would also be able to see them.
3. I had also planned to have a minor, but important, operation during that period.

So, remembering what I had learnt about project management, I sought to apply it to the situation with enthusiasm.

First, I identified the overall goals of the total project. These were:

- to deal with *all* the management issues thrown at me by the ICI situation without letting *any* balls drop;
- to achieve the handover smoothly and, if possible, to move on in four to five months rather than in six, and especially, to *avoid the project lasting longer than six months*;
- to learn a lot in the process, and to (justifiably) add to my CV that I had been a senior line manager at ICI;
- to find a job elsewhere in the process;
- to avoid undue disruption to my family;
- to avoid disrupting my final MBA exams (which I took five weeks into the secondment).

I had taken the important project management principle on board: 'Manage backwards from the project objectives.'

My second step was to do a thorough diagnosis of the current situation. This in itself was reasonably complex and required a mini-project in its own right. This was completed by the end of Week 1. An associated mini- (soft) project was to establish credibility with my own team (who admitted some weeks later in the pub that they had been 'waiting for me to fall over' – not that I gave them any opportunity).

At this juncture I reasoned that besides establishing a project plan overall for the next four to five months, the main priority was to improve the morale of my team. I felt that unless I did this, I would not have sufficient resources to be able to address the mountain of work associated with both acquisitions and with the ICI three-year plan (and associated R&D project appraisals).

Intuitively, I had therefore identified the soft critical path of activities which I would need to manage to stand a good chance of success.

Although my team did not (at that point) feel concerned about the three-year plan, I decided we needed to create a project plan for that process in detail, with key activities, outputs and milestones. My staff were a little surprised at my insistence on this point at first, until they reflected that the previous year the planning inputs had been late and needed re-work, causing a last-minute panic of considerable magnitude.

The three-year plan was all I needed – just at the time when the acquisitions-hungry management team went in search of prey in September, following the summer holidays.

I was also wary of the near-certainty of making another acquisition during the summer months as I knew this would generate significant integration work into early autumn. And, in addition to this, I had a slightly uncomfortable feeling about some transfer pricing issues which were beginning to bubble up in the UK. I had had some (limited) experience of transfer pricing disputes from the past when I worked in a French company. I felt that the people at ICI were likely to be much nicer about sorting this (a key project assumption) but human beings are fickle, and I was liable to be disappointed.

So, after the first four weeks the following had occured:

- We had successfully put in place a project plan to cover the next four months of activity.
- We had successfully put in place a detailed plan for the three-year plan – which was now being implemented.
- The morale of my team was very good and there was a definite sense of purpose and confidence; one of my junior reports even had a suspected ulcer – but this turned out to be psychosomatic – but this now became a counselling project.
- The UK acquisition had fallen by the board, but was now replaced by the smaller acquisition target. This had begun my New Project Number One.
- The first quarter's management reporting (a mini-project) had highlighted that US operations had major performance problems. New Project Number Two was to investigate this situation. New Project Number Five was the conceived re-appraisal of the business's R&D projects – which required review due to changed assumptions about future market opportunities.
- I had visited the new acquisition in Europe and highlighted the action areas in management reporting and planning.
- A possible new project for the Scandinavian acquisition target had appeared. I talked our top management out of proceeding with this on the grounds that (a) Was it really attractive/did it fit our strategy? (b) Would we be able to do it and integrate it effectively? (c) Would it be credible to put a business case for this acquisition to Group Head Office at a time when our credibility had taken something of a hammering. This new project was put on ice.
- New Project Number Three was to sort out the transfer pricing problem.
- New Project Number Four was to deal with integration issues around the (now consummated) small UK acquisition.

New Project Number Five was the re-appraisal of the businesses R&D projects which required review, given the changed assumptions about future market prospects. In addition to these projects, I did move my family down to the ICI locality (at least over the summer holidays) and I had the surgery I had planned. Interestingly, I had not been fully informed by my doctor that it would take me a week to fully recover from the surgery. During meetings to discuss the potential Scandinavian acquisition, I felt myself slumping under the table with pain (in fact I could have used a number of ICI's drugs to sort this out!). It is just possible, I do not know, that this helped me be even more challenging that normal in questioning that project, helping me to avoid a weekend in Denmark, which was a lot less attractive to me than other members of the management team.

But as we shall see later on, personal agendas can and do play an enormous (if unspoken) role in dictating the direction and outcome of business projects.

I had also to plan for 'Acts of God'. I left a week's 'float' (or spare) time to accommodate unseen eventualities during the three-year plan process. By coincidence, just before the time we submitted our plan we experienced a hurricane (yes, this was an *official* hurricane). I awoke one morning to find trees blown over everywhere. Power was down for ten days. Pubs ran out of food, computers did not work, spreadsheets did not happen. Nevertheless, we made the deadline whilst ICI Global Technology did not (I confess that we had a back-up power supply, whilst they did not).

Despite the flurry of work, which through project management became a more steady and well-directed process, I was also able to find another job as a consultant. ICI immediately offered me my next project there – I declined, because of the very clear objectives which I laid out earlier.

Besides the foreseeable and the emergent projects I also undertook one final one – New Project Number Five became one to set up acquisition process (pre, during and post the deal).

I now look back on that six-month period in ICI Biosciences not only with fondness but also with much gratitude for the learning which I took away from it. More specifically, we can distil 11 key learning lessons for project management from it, as follows:

1. Diagnose each pharma project sufficiently, especially the reasons why there are problems. What are you looking to get out of it, what are the overall deliverables?
2. What options are available to create these deliverables?
3. What further projects (or mini-projects) will also be required to reach these deliverables?
4. What key taken-for-granted assumptions have you made, and what could go wrong, when and how, if these are not fulfilled?
5. Be prepared to say 'no' to projects (or sub-projects) which are either not fundamentally attractive or are too difficult – given your resources or other reasons, or both.
6. Do not skimp on mini-projects (such as improving team morale) that are on the 'soft' critical path.

7. Recognise new projects for what they are (for example, transfer pricing was sufficiently complex to be called a 'project').

8. For each and every project, anticipate ahead of the activity the likely *value* that it will create.

9. Position each part of the project effectively within the organisation so that it gets the attention it deserves.

10. Recognise that personal agendas of both yourself and of others have to be identified and managed, too.

11. Managing complex and difficult projects in the pharma industry involves anticipating all kinds of factors not often thought relevant to project management, like personal health, working away from home, prioritising one's job load as a bundle of projects, and even acting as a counsellor to your team.

My experience in this technologically complex environment highlights the fluidity, open-endedness and apparent unpredictability of pharma business projects. Not only do they expand or contract in scope currently, but they can appear to veer off in new directions or at tangents.

Their critical paths are also not at all obvious as there are many choices in the order in which one conducts activities. This order is not merely determined by what has to be done purely in operational sequence, but there are also *political* priorities to be sorted. (Observing and working with pharma managers might suggest that political sequencing is *the* most important way of organising project activities.)

The experience at ICI Biosciences therefore demonstrates the utility of a number of project management techniques within the pharma industry. These include:

- defining the project (or projects) – both at a business and personal level;

- initial definition of project scope and interdependencies;

- targeting the deliverables (or, in more traditional language, the 'results');

- identifying the key activities (or sub-projects);

- planning and managing timescales;

- mobilising resources.

But in addition to these more traditional aspects of project management, we also see the importance of:

- thorough problem diagnosis;

- looking at a diversity of options – not only for *which* projects to do but *how* to do them (especially vis-à-vis acquisitions);

- managing stakeholders – those individuals with an interest in and an influence on the project;

- dealing with uncertainty;

- trading-off not merely tangible but also less tangible value;

- creating a strategic vision for the project (that is, to complete the ICI project without annoying my family and whilst still finding a job elsewhere);

- identifying key implementation difficulties.

The above areas reach beyond the domain of traditional project management, carrying us explicitly into the land of strategy, finance and organisational analysis, and into a more contemporary process for project management which is more ideally suited to the pharma industry. Many pharma projects may seem to be 'mission impossible' ones with hindsight, but these projects are full of learning lessons as we hope you will see in the next exercise.

EXERCISE – MANAGING A 'MISSION IMPOSSIBLE' PROJECT IN THE PAST

Reflect on one project you were involved with in the past, which appeared (with perhaps the benefit of hindsight) to be a 'mission impossible' project and ask yourself:

- Was this imposed upon you, or did you actively allow yourself to get involved in it?
- Did you sense this as a 'mission impossible' project at an early stage – and what signals gave you the clue?
- Did you actively consider more radical options for the project's strategy before the difficulties began to become insurmountable (for example, to do it very differently, or even to not do it at all)?
- Did you call for help, or did you try to soldier on on your own?
- Overall, what were the key learnings from this project? (Consider things which you would do differently, again, or not do at all.)

The Pharmaceutical Project Management Process

The pharma project management process (which we now introduce) contains five key stages (see Figure 1.2). These stages include:

1. defining the project;

2. creating the project strategy;

3. detailed project planning;

4. implementation and control;

5. review and learning.

Figure 1.2 emphasises that project management may require the project to be redefined or the project strategy to be revisited. It also highlights the need to anticipate the project's implementation difficulty – at the planning stage and even earlier.

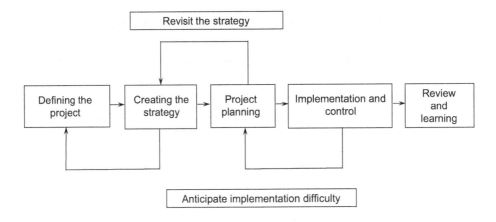

Figure 1.2   The pharmaceutical project management process

Defining the project involves:

- diagnosing any key problems, opportunities or other needs which gave rise to the project in the first place: for example, inadequate IT systems to document clinical trials;

- defining the project's scope and main focus; for example, which countries/patient segments should a clinical trial focus on?

- clarifying any key interdependencies, for example, between or during drug development projects;

- creating an overall vision for the project, and its defining key objectives: for example, what market share for a new drug are we really targeting?

- thinking through, at least initially, who the stakeholders might be – for example, what are the media's attitudes going to be to a particular clinical trial?

The above reveals that defining the pharma project is not something which is done in five minutes – and that this definition is frequently not self-evident. Project definition involves a good deal of reflection about the purpose and the context of the project.

Next, creating the project strategy for the pharma project entails:

- exploring the external and internal environment for the project in greater depth;

- defining the key strategic goals of the project more specifically;

- examining strategic options for (a) what to do, and (b) how to do it, including 'push' versus 'pull' strategies (a 'push' strategy is one where little discretion is allowed to those stakeholders impacted on by the project; a 'pull' strategy is one where the degree of discretion is higher, either over the project's goals or the project's process, or both);

- a preliminary appraisal of the project's overall attractiveness and implementation difficulty;

- further thinking about the positioning of its key stakeholders, and how these might be influenced.

Project strategy thus demands even more thought than project definition – as there may be many ways of implementing the project.

Detailed project planning requires:

- a detailed analysis of the key activities and/or sub-projects which the overall project strategy requires;

- an analysis of how these activities are networked in a sequence, given their interdependencies and also an analysis of their critical paths (see Chapter 4);

- an appraisal of key uncertainties along with contingency plans and impact analysis;

- a financial appraisal of the project's value and cost drivers, along with an overview of the financials ('value drivers' are those project variables which will add directly or indirectly to its positive cash flow potential, whilst 'cost drivers' will detract from this).

Whilst this is the core of traditional project management, project plans will only ever be as good as the project strategies they are based upon.

Implementation and control now necessitates:

- thorough definition of project milestones and responsibilities;

- key implementation difficulties being previously highlighted and counter-measures already built-in to ensure that resource and action plans are adequate;

- some forward thinking about the likely dynamics of the project over time.

- Implementation and control thus requires continual checking back to the project's strategy and also its vision – to ensure that apparent delivery of milestones is actually fulfilling the original purpose of the project.

Finally, the review and learning stage involves:

- revisiting the project to assess whether the targeted deliverables were achieved, whether the implementation process went smoothly or not, how effectively was the project positioned politically, and also other behavioural lessons;

- looking at how could the project management process itself be improved.

Review and learning is thus not merely a peripheral part of the process, but is the driver of continuous improvement in the project process. Generally speaking, review and learning is frequently the weakest link in the project management chain. For example, we have found in the pharma industry relatively few R&D research projects, particularly clinical research, are subjected to a formal learning review. This is even though they are frequently not completed on time, and this may result in delays costing millions of dollars of revenue. This does appear to be a very real weakness, which ought to be remedied.

Given that the pharma project management process is frequently not idyllic, try this exercise in order to tease out some of the strengths and weaknesses of your past processes.

EXERCISE – DIAGNOSING STRENGTHS AND WEAKNESSES OF YOUR PAST PHARMA PROJECT PROCESS

For one past pharma project in which you have been involved ask yourself:

- How well were the following aspects of the process managed?
- If you were to give a score (out of 100) for each of the five stages of the project, what would this give you overall?
- To what extent did earlier stage deficiencies (for example, defining the project or creating the project strategy) detract from later stages, for example, implementation and control?

Conclusion

Managing pharma projects demands far more than merely traditional project management techniques. In addition, such complex projects demand a considerable skill in strategic thinking. This strategic thinking is required at all stages of the project, but particularly in the first two stages of pharma project management:

- defining the project;

- creating the project strategy;

and also, at its final stage:

- review and learning.

In the next chapter we will take this theme further by investigating the key links between pharma projects and business strategy.

But, before we move on, check that you have actually devoted sufficient time to doing the exercises in this first chapter. This will help you to get full value from the book as it proceeds and will also establish a good learning process for the rest of your reading. If you *did not* work on the exercises as you were reading, then just spend 20–25 minutes doing this now.

2

Linking Pharmaceutical Projects with Business Strategy

Introduction

Pharma companies have been going through a number of major changes as their environment has shifted – especially over the last decade. These shifts have had a profound impact on the environment under which projects are undertaken. The major external shifts in the industry and its environment are:

- Technological advances in healthcare combined with an ageing population have put up the total cost of healthcare (especially to governments), which has put pressure on prices, and encouraged the prescription of generic drugs.

- Regulatory requirements have intensified, making it more costly to develop and test drugs, and launch them to market. This has also made it more difficult to achieve project timeliness.

- These pressures have encouraged many mergers in the industry, which have led to many restructuring, cost reduction and culture change projects.

If we add into this the increasing strains of the public sector to afford growth in the drugs bill – especially post credit crunch and without the economic growth we saw up until 2008 – then the effects of this crisis will be passed on to the pharma sector over the next five years. As we saw in the Preface, we will also see changes in the rollout of drug discoveries which will mute the effects of the traditional blockbuster drug.

Pharma companies have tried to respond to these pressures by looking to project management processes to help accelerate projects (whether clearly developmental, marketing or changes in infrastructure), and to reduce costs. But often these project management processes have not been up to the challenges posed by the shifts which we outlined earlier, especially because:

- they have been applied mechanistically from engineering and construction contexts, without recognition of the greater uncertainty (and sometimes even fuzziness) surrounding pharma projects;

- they are frequently not well prioritised;

- they result in resources being spread too thinly.

Many of these causes are directly or indirectly attributable to the fact that projects are often not well linked to the business strategy, an issue to which we now turn in this second chapter.

Defining Strategy

In many pharma organisations business projects are only loosely connected to the bigger picture of the business strategy. This may be a variety of reasons for this. First, those at the project level may not be fully aware of the business strategy itself, except in a most general way. Top management might be reluctant to share this picture out of concern for commercial sensitivity (especially in terms of future direction), or because they may wish to reserve power centrally, or for political reasons. Also, the project managers themselves may not see it as so important that they are aware of the detailed and specific content of the business strategy.

Second, the strategy itself may not be clear and worked out in detail. Whilst it may contain some strategic thinking, these ideas may not be fully integrated, mutually consistent or worked through. Sadly, it is rather hard to link one thing (a project) to another thing (a business strategy) if the second thing only half exists.

Not only might the content of the strategy be unclear but the very meaning of 'strategy' may itself be ambiguous. 'Business strategy' is a much-used but also much-abused term. For instance, in one major multinational pharma company literally scores of managers had the word 'strategy' in their job titles. But no one had actually even defined what the word meant.

A conventional definition (definition A) of the word 'strategy' is:

> *The means of getting from where you are now to where you want to be –*
> *and with competitive advantage.*

This definition is useful in that it emphasises the need to know where you are – and to know this intimately first – before deciding both where you want to be and how to get there with competitive advantage. This definition is very much one of a 'deliberate strategy' (Mintzberg, 1994), that is one based on a well-articulated design to match the organisation and its aspirations with its present and future environment.

A more stretching, and in some ways superior definition (definition B) of strategy is:

> *The intuitive sense, not of where the business actually is but where it*
> *ought to be, and of what needs to happen to bring about this ideal state.*

Increasingly we prefer definition B to definition A as it justly emphasises the more creative and imaginative role of strategy. In Mintzberg's terms (Mintzberg, 1994) it is more of a 'visionary strategy'.

One way of remembering that strategy is about the 'ought' rather than merely about the 'is', is to think of it in a way reminiscent of the Spice Girls pop group, successful world-wide in the 1990s, who coined the slogan:

> *What do I really, really, really want?*

So, 'strategy' could be defined as:

> *Strategy is what we really, really, really want.*

But, strategy needs to be more than aspirational. Turning now to our third definition of strategy (the 'Spice Girl Approach'), in order to appreciate the significance of this idea, try the next exercise:

EXERCISE – THE VISIONARY PHARMACEUTICAL PROJECT

Think now of one project in which you are involved – either in business or in your personal life, ask yourself the following:

- As currently formulated, does the project give you an average result, aimed at merely removing some worst aspects of a problem?
- Or does it receive its inspiration from 'What you really, really, want?'
- And, if the latter, how does this inspiration drive all of your thinking about the project strategy and its resource plans?

Our next definition of 'strategy' is again a humorous one. The definition is quite simple:

Strategy is the cunning plan.

The idea of the 'cunning plan' comes from the British television comedy series, *Blackadder*. Here the character Baldrick always reminds us of the need to think up 'a cunning plan' when the characters get themselves into situations of insurmountable difficulty.

More formally, we can define the word 'cunning' as 'clever, innovative and surprising' and the 'cunning plan' as 'a new combination of ideas for achieving a project result in surprisingly less time or cost, or with a surprisingly better result'.

In many respects, the second and third definitions of strategy are the most helpful ones to pharma managers. While not claiming to be of high conceptual concept, the 'Spice Girls' and 'cunning plan' approaches to strategy are ones that can be remembered more easily – and applied, too – on a day-to-day basis.

When we have used the notion of a 'cunning plan' in the pharma industry over the past five years initially we are typically met with scepticism. However, invariably it becomes possible to devise quicker ways of achieving project goals – and sometimes at a lower cost and with a better result. It appears that in the pharma industry project timescales (as imposed) are seen as givens, and do not require appropriate challenge.

We now explore in more depth the variety of strategies that exist. First, this highlights the diverse nature of business strategy, for if we are to link pharma projects successfully to business strategies then we must most surely examine the very nature of those business strategies first. We do this by examining what we call the strategy mix and its impact at the project level.

Second, we examine the impact of incremental thinking on projects, and how this can create as less favourable environment for the project and how this can be diagnosed.

Third, we turn explicitly to the role which project management can play in supporting pharma breakthrough thinking and advantage.

Fourth, we will look at how business strategy can be looked at more dynamically as a stream of projects. Whilst strategy is – in practice – often made incrementally, rather than seeing this a threat to strategic planning (as does Mintzberg, 1994), we can now see *the project* as being an important unit of strategic analysis.

The Strategy Mix

Besides the more rational models of strategy (known as 'deliberate' strategy), we can also have ones which are more fluid, or 'emergent'. Mintzberg has defined this (emergent) strategy as being one of: 'A pattern in a stream of decisions or actions.' Our contact with numerous pharma clients leads us to conclude that whilst there may be a very high level 'deliberate' strategy for the business, and there may well be deliberate project-level objectives, at this project level the strategy is often still emergent.

Whilst many 'decisions' or 'actions' may not be identified as projects, certainly if they are truly 'strategic' then they ought to be projects, whether this is made explicit or implicit. For if we go back to the classic definition of a 'project', which is:

> A project is a complex set of activities with a predefined result which is targeted over a particular time and to a specific cost.

then strategic decisions (or actions) in the pharma industry are necessarily projects.

This point that 'business strategy' is effectively a collection of mutually aligned projects designed to create a specific competitive positioning is a most important and helpful one. It is important because it shifts much of our frame of reference in strategic management from the 'very big picture', indeed, to the more tangible and management level. In effect, this recognises that most strategic thinking should be done at a smaller scale level than is typically appreciated. We call this level that of the 'mini-strategy'. This approach is helpful because it enables management (at all levels) to get a better grip on pharma business strategy, especially so that they *actually get on and implement it.*

Whilst Mintzberg's extension of the types of strategy from one to two (deliberate and now emergent) is laudable, these two forms simply do not go far enough. We have therefore added three additional forms: the submergent, the 'emergency' and the 'detergent'), giving:

- deliberate;

- emergent;

- submergent;

- emergency;

- detergent.

These forms of strategy are depicted in Figure 2.1 which shows a deliberate strategy at the start, often moving into an emergent phase. Unless its duration and implementation is steered, it may drift into submergent or 'emergency' phases, or even 'detergent' (where it is tidied up).

A 'submergent' strategy is a deliberate or an emergent strategy which has ceased to work. In this phase managers often re-double their efforts, putting in more time and resource without questioning the original scope of the project and the basis of the project strategy.

An 'emergency' strategy is one where there is so little coherence to action that there is no real sense of direction at all.

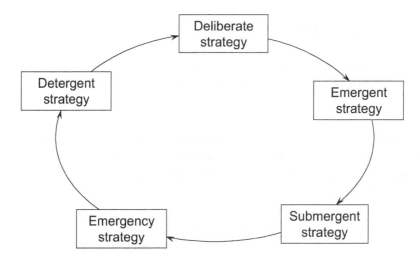

Figure 2.1   The strategy mix

Finally, a 'detergent' strategy is one where a strategy which has not worked in the past is now being re-thought, and its various parts which did not work in the past are being discarded, or changed.

Any pharma strategy (or project) can be analysed to discern which stage of its evolution it is presently at. A strategy or project which is in two or more of the above phases simultaneously is said to have a 'strategy mix'.

Besides asking oneself where the business strategy and the project strategy is, vis-à-vis the strategy mix, it is also imperative to examine the strategy mix as it changes over time. Taking a typical pharma example of a major change project or programme we see the following: initially there is an intensive phase of deliberate strategy but quite quickly this opens out into a number of emergent strategies. Some of these project strategies fan out, losing their sense of direction and thus becoming 'submergent' or even 'emergency' strategies.

Opening it out just a little bit more, now let us imagine the patchwork of strategy existing within a pharma organisation. At any one time there could be a very clear, deliberate strategy in some business units, whilst others are far more emergent, some submergent/emergency, and one or two are actually detergent. At the corporate level there could be a largely detergent strategy. Then there might be some key organisational projects going on either within or across business units. Some of these may be start-up, deliberate projects. Others might be mature but still 'deliberate' projects. There might also be some highly emergent projects and some (sadly) submergent projects. The result is therefore one of a confusing patchwork of strategy – giving rise to inevitable cynicism.

Does this sound like your own pharma company? Possibly. The cost of this patchwork could be very significant in terms of a lack of focus for resource allocation and for project prioritisation, and also for a blunting of organisational energy and enthusiasm.

The 'strategy mix' is thus a helpful way of visualising more about how a project may evolve over time within its changing environment.

The strategy mix can be used for diagnosis at a number of levels, for example for pharma projects at the:

- corporate strategy level;

- business strategy level;

- breakthrough programme level (that is, involving a number of interdependent projects which will combine to support the business strategy);

- project level itself.

A key conclusion from the idea of the 'strategy mix' is that no single form of strategy is therefore appropriate to managing pharma projects in different contexts. Deliberate, emergent (and even detergent) project strategies need to be managed together – and in a skilful juggling act.

The above forms of strategy are all extremely important to business projects as (a) the strategy mix may be predominately of an emergent, submergent or emergency nature, meaning that it is very difficult, if not impossible, to make linkages between the project and its higher level business strategy, and (b) the project strategy itself may be in a more emergent, submergent or 'emergency' state. Although this is clearly undesirable, it is by no means an inconceivable state. Many projects lack sufficient clarity of purpose and inherent advantage to actually succeed.

For instance, there have been occasions when pharma companies have developed drugs and even reached phase III before realising there was an insufficient net present value from the resultant with cash flows to be able to gain an adequate return on investment.

Where the business strategy is very fluid it is then that much harder to engender a logic and clarity at the project level. Equally, where key business projects have the habit of not being terribly well thought through, then there is perhaps an even greater tendency for the business strategy to become fuzzy and ill-thought through.

Before we leave the strategy mix for a while, let us do a brief recap.

First, the various levels of strategy in pharma companies are often loosely interconnected, meaning that it is not often straightforward to link projects with business strategy. Second, the business strategy itself might be fluid and ambiguous. Third, the business strategy might be at a lower point in the strategy mix cycle (a blend of submergent, emergency or detergent strategies) and here there will be very little to link pharma projects back to. Fourth, different projects themselves might be at a different phase of their own strategy mix: some may be mainly deliberate or emergent, or perhaps mainly at the submergent/emergency phases, or maybe mainly detergent.

All of these factors account (in large part) for the fluidity of projects and their susceptibility to change within pharma companies. To understand this problem a little more let us turn now to the role of incrementalism.

The Role of Incrementalism

In this section we look at some of the practical aspects of strategic decision-making in the pharma industry. One of the most difficult issues which pharma companies face is setting a drug development strategy. As we have already seen, 'deliberate' strategies – if well thought through – are more appropriate then looser, more emergent strategies.

The mind-set of many managers in the pharma industry on the way in which projects are managed is that of a very rational and integrated framework and process. But organisational reality is frequently very different from this.

Let us therefore, first look quickly at the role of 'incrementalism' in project management.

There has been a long tradition of within both strategic management and organisational theory in emphasising to the importance messier characteristics of the decision process for projects. Braybrook and Lindblom (1963), for instance, described decision-making in organisations as 'disjointed incrementalism' in the sense that decisions are taken in semi-isolation from each other, producing a disjointed pattern of strategic thinking and action. March and Simon (1958) more crudely called this syndrome 'The garbage-can model of decision-making' to exaggerate its apparent randomness. Quinn (1980) more kindly described it as 'logical incrementalism' to reflect the fact that new decisions (and equally, therefore, strategic business projects) get overlaid, in as logical a way as possible, to the existing mess.

Again, many managers in pharma companies will respond intuitively with an 'A-ha...' to these descriptions, especially that of Quinn, who gave ample recognition to the limited rationality which nevertheless occurs in management. But even where there is a predominance of incrementalism, this does not mean that it has to be that haphazard.

We can therefore distinguish between 'haphazard' incrementalism (as per the incrementalist school of decision-making) and a more visionary version of 'enlightened' incrementalism. In enlightened incrementalism managers *do* try to work to an overall vision for not only individual projects but also for project programmes and for the business strategy itself. But, at the same time, they are equally mindful not only of the specifics of the current project opportunity but also of their pharma project's legacy – based on other projects or initiatives in the organisation, both past and present. This historical legacy is almost inevitably going to be a result of post-incrementalism. Whilst taking this inevitability on board, project managers do need to continually go back to 'what do we really, really, want?' – and therefore their 'Spice Girls' approach.

In this section we now look at some of the practical aspects of strategic decision-making in the pharma industry. One of the most difficult issues which pharma companies have is setting a drug development strategy. As we have already seen, 'deliberate' strategies – if well thought through – are more appropriate than looser, more emergent strategies.

To get a better handle on the causes of incrementalism, let us examine next how the internal competitive environment of the project impacts on its development and positioning.

PROJECT DECISION-MAKING AND THE DELIBERATE STRATEGY

In drug development we see a close fusion between strategic decision making and project management. The pharma industry is continually looking at ways to decrease the time to bring a drug to the market. It is estimated that the current average time to develop a drug is 12 years and that this may be reduced by three years with the successful use of project management.

A central part of the drug development strategy is to set clear objectives for the development and lifecycle management of the drug. Most drug candidates do not make it onto the market and typically you start with 10,000 compounds which are screened in drug discovery, of which 250 may enter pre-clinical development. Of these, ten will go into clinical trials and only one will come on the market. So the vast majority of compounds will fail to get on the market. Therefore, it is imperative in the pharma industry to fail fast and not to continue the development of a compound which is not going to get to the market.

Planning and managing the clinical trial programmes is the most expensive and time-consuming part of developing a drug. In particular, overseeing international clinical trial programmes is a central part of running clinical trials and thus needs good project management tools. Many pharma companies have developed in-house project management systems or have purchased commercial systems to plan, manage development programmes and track the progress of studies. Contract Research Organisations (CROs) also use such systems to manage projects and to keep their clients informed of progress.

It is easy to become emotionally attached to the compounds in development and it is not unusual for drugs to be allowed to continue in development when the 'no-go' decision should have been reached (or what we call earlier, the 'detergent strategy'). It is often a difficult decision to stop developing a drug but it may be equally essential to do this.

Using the Target Product Profile (TPP) (or 'product profile' or 'project targeted profile' – or something similar) is a good way to help make 'go/no-go' decisions (which correspond with our 'deliberate strategy') since it establishes clear criteria that the compound must meet in order for it to be developed. The purpose of go/no-go criteria is to decide whether to continue to developing the drug or not.

Given the considerable cost, particularly of the phase III programmes, it is critical to try to halt the development of drugs which will not be a success as quickly as possible. Go/no-go criteria are essential to make these decisions, and phase II is a key point to make this decision. Many companies are now expanding their phase I programmes to do more proof of confidence studies where patients are investigated for efficacy using surrogate endpoints to give a feel for whether it is worth carrying on the development of a drug before going into a traditional phase II study.

Lead compounds have a high failure rate s pharma companies normally have back-up lead candidates in drug discovery which they can develop when a compound meets the no-go criteria. Some companies who are resource rich may develop several lead compounds in the same class in parallel track to save time (possibly two to three years). However, this approach will potentially give a stronger competitive position in the marketplace.

The TPP now provides us with the key template for preparing the development plan. It provides the criteria which the compound must meet in order for it to be successfully commercialised. The TPP should be produced with input from a variety of disciplines involved in the drug development process, including marketing. Carrying out market research and developing a marketing strategy are crucial. This includes an assessment of key competitor compounds in development. Some of the key marketing considerations regarding the likely impact of the product (and therefore revenue forecasts) will be based on edidemiology, alternative treatment options, pricing, margins, market segmentation and expected market penetration rate over time.

It is important to start with the project end in mind and therefore to draw up the basics of the Summary of Product Characteristics (SPC) or data sheet (that is, the hoped for promotional claims, the labelling, in other words, how the product will be prescribed and the indication, the patients to be treated and the purpose of treatment on which the TPP will be based).

The TPP will also be contingent on changes in medical practice, and on the competitive environment – for example, a competitor launching a similar drug to the one we have in development – and on other external as well as internal factors. There have been many examples where the development of a drug has not been based on this criteria and therefore millions of dollars have been wasted. This lack of commercial awareness may result in companies being less profitable and may also make them more vulnerable to being taken over.

Frequently drug candidates/lead compounds will be considered for development in more than one therapeutic indication. Therefore it will be necessary to produce a TPP for each indication. Usually a decision will be made to select one particular TPP option for development, although parallel development will be carried out for some compounds.

In terms of managing a portfolio of potential compounds to develop it is essential to use criteria to decide which TPP to develop. Such criteria include the economic potential such as likely return on investment, feasibility (likelihood of technical success, ease of meeting the target label claims, and clinical and regulatory success, that is, probability of clinical efficacy and safety success) and time to reach the market. It is also important to take into account the country or regional differences since the TPP may need to reflect this – for example, different routes or methods of drug administration may be preferred in some countries.

A CHECKLIST OF ITEMS TO CONSIDER INCLUDING IN THE TARGET PRODUCT PROFILE:

The following items are useful to think through when creating the TTP document.

1.   The development candidate code number.

2.   The therapeutic indication.

3.   The safe pharmacology profile acceptable including safety pharmacology of metabolites.

4.   The manufacturing process acceptable including:

a)   ability to produce commercial scale product;

b)   acceptable stability of clinical formulation and final formulation.

5.   The efficacy – minimum required.

6.   The safety risk/benefit ratio – this may include considerations for no major side effects, no major contraindications, not to have a narrow therapeutic window.

7.   The administration convenience – for example, once-a-day dosage, easy to administer, preferably oral formulation which is palatable to patients.

8.   Innovation – new class of compound, significantly different to compounds on the market, first in class (for example, Viagra).

The TPP should then be used as the basis for designing the drug development plan.

KEY ACTIVITIES IN THE DRUG DEVELOPMENT PROJECT PLAN

The following are examples of key activities in the drug development project plan.

Non-clinical (pre-clinical)

- Toxicology studies

    - Acute toxicity
    - Subacute toxicity, two to four weeks in two species
    - Subchronic, three months in two species
    - Chronic toxicity, for example, six months in two species
    - Reproduction studies
        ~ Embryotoxicity
        ~ Fertility
        ~ Perinatal toxicity
    - Oncognenicity (carcinogenicity)
    - Mutagegicity

- Pharmacokinetic studies
- Absorption, distribution, metabolism, excretion (ADME) in two species

Clinical Development

- Phase I (human pharmacology)

  - Single and multiple dose
  - Bioequivalence studies
  - Interaction studies
  - Special populations, for example, renal, hepatic impairment, the elderly, children

- Phase II (therapeutic exploritary)

  - Dose finding

- Phase III (therapeutic confirmatory)

  - Efficacy studies – at least two studies

- Phase IV (therapeutic use)

  - Post Marketing Surveilance (PMS)

Manufacturing

- Clinical trial supply manufacturing

- Formulation (phase I formulation may be different to later phases)

- Full scale-up of commercial product

- Stability testing

- Substance characterisation

- Formulation characterisation

Regulatory considerations

- Can investigational New Drug (IND) for Food and Drug Administration (FDA) submission and EU Clinical Trial Directive submission requirements be met?

- Can New Drug Application (FDA requirements), Marketing Authorisation Application (MAA) (EU requirements), and International Conference of Harmonisation (ICH) Common Technical Document for approving a drug be met?

- Can any other regulatory or guidelines requirements can be met, whether international or national, including requirements for Good Clinical Practice (GCP) and ethical or Institutional Review Board (IRB) approval? It is essential to identify all relevant guidelines and regulations relevant to the compound in development. For example, there are now many regulations and guidelines both FDA and from Europe for many therapeutic areas. If these are not followed this may prevent a company from obtaining a regulatory approval to market a drug until the guidelines/regulations have been met.

The key lesson from the above list is that drug development projects are quite diverse and therefore require individual and highly specific project strategies.

Understanding the Internal Competitive Environment

Stepping back from more detailed systems considerations, let us now look at the internal competitive context which pharma projects find themselves in.

The causes of incrementalism (which we discussed earlier) can now be understood better using a picture adapted from Michael Porter's five forces competitive model (for competitive environments – see Figure 2.2). To the very left of the figure we see the legacy from past projects. To the centre we see competitive rivalry with existing projects. To the right we see *future* projects – which might either be supported by this project or potentially might need to be forgone if we do this particular project.

To the top of the figure we see projects which are interdependent with this one – and which are likely to suffer if this one does not go ahead. And to the very bottom we see substitute projects.

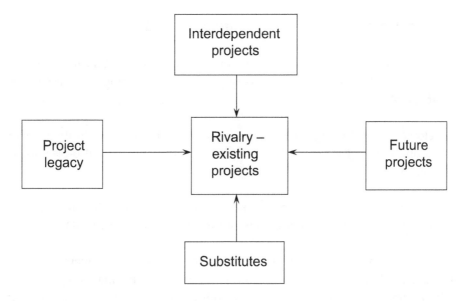

Figure 2.2   Project forces analysis

Not only does this model explain the potentially negative impact of incrementalism but it also helps diagnose the project's organisational environment.

For instance, a pharma project which scores:

*** high fit with future projects;

*** high synergies with interdependent projects;

*** low rivalry with other projects;

*** low threat with substitute projects (other ways of doing the same thing);

*** a lack of legacy of past projects

is going to have a particularly favourable project environment. Conversely, one which scores poorly on these five forces criteria is likely to have a very rough ride.

Project Programmes, Interdependencies and Breakthroughs

A key lesson from our earlier section on incrementalism is that it is likely to be extremely difficult to manage every project within a single process of the 'strategic plan'.

However, by forcing the organisation to be more selective in its focus of attention, there is greater likelihood of being able to turn initial project ideas into real action.

To achieve this, 'breakthrough management' now comes to our rescue, as used for many years for instance at SmithKline Beecham (now GSK).

Business projects are often seen by managers as relatively separate activities, unlinked to one another, but in reality many business projects form part of bigger programmes which in turn form a central part of the business strategy. These linkages between projects will be much stronger where there is a relatively clear and primarily 'deliberate' business strategy. Very substantial and important projects (or clusters of projects) can thus aptly be called 'breakthrough projects'. A breakthrough project is defined as:

> *A project which will have a material impact on either the business's external competitive edge, its internal capabilities or its financial performance – or all three.*

The idea of 'breakthrough' comes from the Japanese philosophy of HOSHIN, or 'breakthrough management', which is an increasingly well-recognised management technique. SmithKline Beecham (now GSK) has used the 'HOSHIN' process now for many years.

HOSHIN has a particularly great appeal in high technology markets principally, we believe, because it helps managers in pharma companies to prioritise. HOSHIN actually prescribes that only a really small number of 'breakthrough' projects or programmes should be attempted at any one time in a particular business area. The absolute maximum of these projects is three, and the minimum is one.

By restricting the number of 'breakthrough' projects to a minimum, the following advantages are likely to accrue:

- critical mass of resources is more likely to be achieved;

- marginal projects will not be undertaken;

- organisational attention and communication will be focused on a much smaller number of things at any one time;

- the organisation is less likely to wear itself out on many very difficult projects.

The advantages of having a very tight number of breakthrough projects significantly outweighs the perceived drawbacks of concerns that three major areas 'is not very much, then'. Further, if it were possible to launch and get reasonably well-bedded-in projects within, say, a six-month time period, then this would permit as many as nine (or three projects within each six months) over, say, an 18-month time period. Each of these 'breakthrough' projects can then be clustered alongside others to which it has the closest similarity, and interdependence with.

Finally, a business strategy can be seen as a stream of projects. This 'group' of projects is not static but represents rather a flow of projects over time – which collectively shifts or transforms the business. An important premise in this book is that strategic management should give its primary attention to managing pharma projects – within an overall strategic vision of the business – rather than to developing comprehensive, catch-all business strategies top-down.

Conclusion

'Strategies' which form the overall framework for managing specific projects are not always very clear and deliberate. Instead they form a 'strategy' mix which will shift over time, moving from deliberate to emergent and back again to deliberate – hopefully without going around the cycle of submergent, emergency and detergent strategies. Or, potentially, it may shift from emergent to submergent and then become an 'emergency' project strategy. Or, it could move through any of these modes and then to 'detergent' – where it is sorted out. Also, projects are an absolutely key vehicle for implementing strategies in the pharma industry as Figure 2.3 shows.

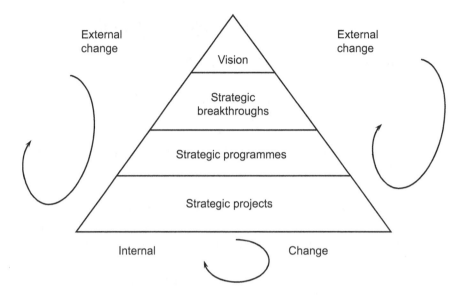

Figure 2.3   Business strategy as a stream of projects

The strategy mix partly accounts for why it may be difficult to link projects with strategy – equally, each individual project may itself move through the strategy mix – starting off with clarity of scope, objectives and linkages (a deliberate strategy) and then slipping into the other phases of the strategy mix.

Turning to the dynamics of strategy, and of pharma projects, we saw that a typical flow of project decisions was highly incremental and fluid. This led to internal rivalry between projects and to somewhat chaotic influences on the trajectory of major projects. Whilst tolerating (to at least some degree) this ambiguity and uncertainty, we needed to establish greater clarity, priority and linkages between projects.

Pharma projects, especially drug development ones are specific and quite diverse. Besides requiring individually tailored project strategies they need quite a lot of systems support, which we have also discussed.

Rather than embracing a comprehensive framework of strategic planning – which would attempt to cope with everything – we then saw breakthrough management as helping to gain a *selective* focus on the really key pharma projects or programmes. This involved management of the key interdependencies between projects.

To illustrate the need for choice in project management, Sun Tzu (1991) said:

> *So when the front is prepared, the rear is lacking, and when the rear is prepared the front is lacking. Preparedness on the left means lack on the right, preparedness on the right means lack on the left. Preparedness everywhere means lack everywhere.*

3

Defining Pharmaceutical Projects

Introduction

Many, but not all pharma industry projects are about drug development. Whilst general project management principles apply to all projects in the industry (technical and non-technical), in drug development projects there are some quite specific considerations which we examine in this chapter.

Defining the project (and its scope) is often the most critical phase of pharma project management, especially for drug development. Unless the problem or opportunity giving rise to the project is thoroughly diagnosed, then it is quite possible to end up with an inappropriate project strategy, and even the wrong project entirely, especially for non-drug development projects. Even for drug development projects the scope of the project (for example, the time, effort and complexity of conducting clinical trials) is often unrealised.

To recap on project management as a whole, we see the following stages in the process:

- Defining the project: What is the scope of the opportunity (or threat)? What are the objectives and possible benefits, costs and risks? (This implies understanding the fit within the overall drug portfolio.) Also, what is its overall implementation difficulty, and who are the key stakeholders?

- Creating the project strategy: What is the external and internal position (to the department or company) and how are these likely to change? What options are available for implementation and how attractive are they versus difficult to implement? Which stakeholders now need to be mobilised to make it happen?

- Detailed project planning: Is the timing good? And (specifically) what resources do we need, and when to deliver a result effectively? (You need to consider here how stretched resources are generally in the company at the present time.)

- Implementation and control: Is implementation proving effective and if not, why not? What new implementation forces and stakeholders have come into play and how might these be handled? Do the original objectives need revisiting and are these more easily met by other projects? (For instance, have the strategic goals for drug development changed or shifted?). If so, what are the costs of refocusing efforts? Is the pharma project on track in terms of its intended competitive, financial, operational and organisational results?

- Review and Learning: Did we achieve what we set out to achieve? If not, what were the factors which we might have controlled, or attempted to influence, but didn't. Were the implementation difficulties (for example, during clinical trials or marketing the drug) much greater than we envisaged and, if so, why?

Typically, pharma managers focus 80 per cent of their efforts on those areas of the project process which carry only 20 per cent of overall importance. The following table graphically illustrates this tendency:

	Time actually spent (%)	Time which should be spent (%)
Definition and diagnosis	2	20
Strategy and planning	10	20
Implementation	80	40
Control and learning	8	20

Source: A. N. Grundy, *Implementing Strategic Change*, Kogan Page, 1993a.

Note the enormous difference in time between what, in an ideal world, it is felt that managers should spent on 'diagnosis' and what they actually spend. Also note the need to spend considerably more time on learning.

So what does diagnosis actually entail? It involves:

- scoping the pharma project;

- defining the key issues;

- identifying the key project objectives;

- anticipating the project's key stakeholders and difficulty.

Scoping the Pharmaceutical Project

One of the major pitfalls facing managers inexperienced in managing pharma projects is underestimating its scope. For example, with clinical research projects it is often the case that the time needed to recruit sufficient patients is much greater than the time budgeted for. The latter problem is often due to over-optimism about the number of patients that a given population of clinicians can provide.

Another example is that IT projects in the pharma industry grow in size – because the technical and regulatory requirements of information processes are sometimes not fully appreciated. This can produce the consequence of delays and cost escalation for the project.

The scope of a project is very much driven by three major factors:

1. size;

2. duration;

3. key interdependencies.

These three variables form the strategic project scope (see Figure 3.1), which can roughly be defined as:

Project size × Duration × Interdependencies

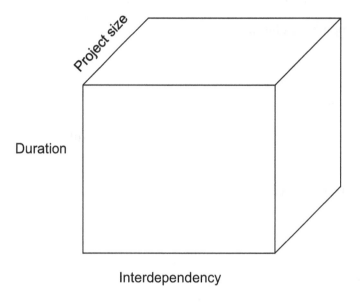

Figure 3.1   Strategic project scope

CASE EXAMPLE – CULTURE CHANGE IN THE PHARMACEUTICAL INDUSTRY

Taking the example of culture change in the pharma industry which began in the early 1990s with the goal of transforming this major organisation, our analysis exposes a rather large project, as follows:

Project Size:

- all of its key business units;
- every level of the organisation: from the chairman down to the operational units;
- worldwide – not local;
- all key management and staff behaviours, and underlying values

Project duration:

- The initial phase was of one year, then follow-up and reinforcement took a further two years. Harvesting the benefits absorbed the next seven years. The total duration of the project was an entire decade, or so.

Project interdependencies;

- performance management;
- training and development;
- career pathing;
- competencies;
- rewards and recognition;
- process re-engineering – administrative;
- process re-engineering – managerial;
- quality management;
- structure change/delayering;
- decentralisation
- strategy development, for example, acquisitions and their integration, divestment;
- managing for shareholder value;
- international management.

The above list appears awesome – and these looks are not deceptive. For this culture change Project was conceived of by its top management team as a deliberate and comprehensive intervention aimed at bringing its management from a more traditional culture set in the 1960s and 70s into the year 2000, and in one leap.

Whilst it could be argued that the giant task might have been broken down further, this would almost certainly have resulted in considerable inefficiencies and inconsistencies across the organisation.

Coming back now to your own practical situation, you are invited to perform the exercise below.

EXERCISE – SCOPING A PROJECT

For a past pharma project in which you have been involved, or one which you are about to become involved in:

- What are the dimensions of its size, especially:
  - which parts of the organisation does it impact upon?
  - how significant is this impact?
  - how different will this impact be in different years?
  - what is the potential scale of investment required?
- What is its likely duration, including:
  - project feasibility study and business case?
  - piloting the project?
  - roll-out?
  - hand-over?
  - reinforcement of any intended changes (for example, in behaviour)?
  - further development?
- What are its key interdependencies:
  - internally, between its various activities?
  - externally, with other projects it supports?
  - externally, with other projects which it might compete with or cut across?

Defining the Key Issues

Our next major step is to diagnose the key issues within a project. This should be done *preferably before* drawing out the project's objectives as we need to explore much more about why we need to look at the project in the first place. This may require a harder look at why current problems exist (for example, with 'fishbone' analysis – see below) or by looking at what visionary strategy might be available by opening up one's imagination (using 'wishbone' or 'from–to' analysis – tools which we discuss later).

Even when we are looking at an R&D project there will still be many project-specific issues which are worthwhile teasing out. Whilst there may be many commonalities, for example, in conducting critical trials, there will always be particular issues associated with the therapeutic characteristics of the drug, its application, of the country in which the trial is tested, the team which is deployed, the availability of patients, and of the timing/resource parameters.

Our key tools for diagnosing the key issues within these projects are therefore as follows:

- fishbone analysis;

- performance drivers;

- wishbone analysis;

- gap analysis;

- from–to analysis

These five techniques serve the following function.

Technique	Applied to	Benefits
Fishbone analysis	Problem diagnosis	Visual and diagnostic
Performance drivers	Performance deficiency diagnosis	Focuses the project on delivering business performance
Wishbone analysis	Opportunity creation	Visual and creative
Gap analysis	Project targeting	Focuses managers' minds on the important
From–to analysis	Project scoping	Scopes the depth and breadth of the project

FISHBONE ANALYSIS

Fishbone (or 'root cause') analysis is an easy way of going behind the more immediate definition of the problem or opportunity. For instance, Figure 3.2 indicates how fishbone analysis can be used to identify why a major pharma company experienced difficulties in the implementation of its strategy.

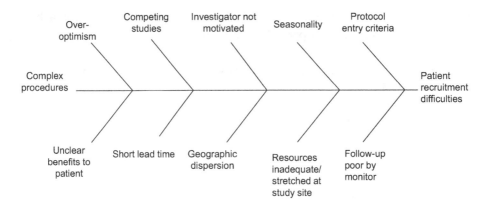

Figure 3.2   Fishbone analysis – patient recruitment

In Figure 3.2 we see the major symptom of the problem drawn at the right-hand side of the page. This is to signify the present situation. We then work backwards to the root causes of the problem. This is exactly the same as 'cause-effect' analysis, except that we are working backwards from a single effect to many causes. Figure 3.2 shows many of the generic causes of difficulties of patient recruitment, a common issue in many, if not most, clinical trials.

Each and every one of the bones of the fishbone can ultimately be traced to its root cause or causes. In fact, fishbone analyses frequently do not fully trace back to these root causes as we are still left with some of the bones at the level of symptoms, so we therefore need to delve deeper to find their root causes.

It is important to flag-up that there is *no particular order* to the bones (or the root causes) of the fishbone. Whilst one bone will probably link on to the next (in the ideas stream), it is likely to hold up the analysis if you try to sort them out as you go. If a group really wants to do this then we suggest that the bones are created using Post-it® notes and these are subsequently resorted and repositioned once the first draft fishbone is complete.

One thing to watch out for when using Fishbone analysis is when several problems masquerade as a single problem. In this case we may well need to split the symptoms out, creating a number of mini-fishbones.

Due to the frequency with which this occurs, we decided to create a new technique, linked to fishbone analysis. This involves drawing an array of smaller fishbones to represent a 'shoal' of problems. As each problem can be quite difficult in its own right, we call this 'piranha' analysis, after that deadly tropical fish which, when part of a large shoal of piranhas, can do serious damage to a human being in a remarkably short period of time.

Many problems in pharma organisations which are the focus of projects are of a very similar kind. Whilst individually they do not amount to all that much, combined or fused with one another they become intractable.

Figure 3.3 represents one such piranha-like problem, namely that of a pharma company which found difficulty in complying with the IT Year 2000 requirements. Whilst the existence of Year 2000 itself was one of the 'symptoms', two other equally important symptoms were: 'IT projects are always late' and 'we are not very good at IT'.

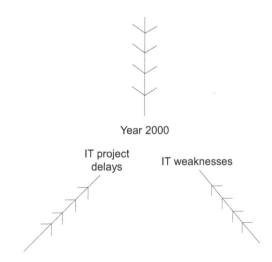

Figure 3.3   Piranha analysis – Year 2000 problem

It is crucial to ensure that you have defined the symptoms of a problem (which is leading to the need for a pharma project) fully, as otherwise you may end up diagnosing and dealing with it only very partially.

Whilst fishbone analysis is most commonly applied to dealing with existing problems, it can also be used in a number of other, and less obvious, ways, especially:

- Anticipating *future* problems or 'things going wrong' with the pharma project, and then working backwards to what caused this to go off the rails.

- Within scenario analysis – to examine the precursors of events which might produce a particular future external or internal environment. These events are often called 'transitional events' in scenario theory – to indicate that they form the transitional link between one state of the world and another. Here we might determine 'the event' – like a particular drug manufacturing problem producing unforeseen side-effects – and then work backwards using fishbone analysis to identify both the *necessary and sufficient causes* of this transitional event.

- To analyse behavioural factors leading up to a particular organisational problem.

- To look at the consequences of the project going wrong. Here we show the fishbone as reversed (a reversed fishbone analysis) with the single cause (a project going wrong) leading on to multi-consequences to the right (see Figure 3.4, which gives an example of this in action).

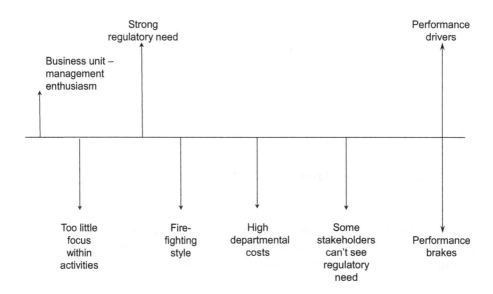

Figure 3.4   Performance driver analysis – regulatory department

Amplifying this final point, it now becomes clearer that fishbone analysis is merely a way of depicting an ongoing cause and effect chain. Here the latter effect becomes a cause of further effects, and so on. The most immediate practical use of reversed fishbone analysis is to identify the more critical interdependencies of the pharma project and to identify the cost of getting it wrong. The cost of possibly project failure is very useful in persuading top management to fully resource the project.

Fishbone analysis should have a particular appeal to pharma professionals with scientific training as it is a very powerful and visual approach to understanding cause and effect relationships in the industry.

In Chapter 4 we will go on to examine how projects can be evaluated and prioritised according to their attractiveness and implementation difficulty (AID analysis). This can also be used to do a very initial prioritisation of which of the various bones of the fishbone are most worthwhile addressing.

Sometimes it is relatively obvious what needs fixing after having performed a fishbone analysis. Sometimes it is easy to see one-for-one solutions for each one of the problem's root causes. Equally, sometimes a number of the bones might be addressed by a single intervention. Ideally, given the limitations and constraints on management time, it may be a better idea to try to solve several issues with one overall solution.

Sometimes it is better still to transcend the entire problem. Rather than trying to manage the situation as it is – and however bad it is – it may be worthwhile looking for an entirely different approach. For example, at a supplier of medical equipment some years ago demonstration stock was causing a major headache as it was becoming increasingly difficult to manage a complex but vitally important flow of trial medical equipment to customers. Equipment had to be tracked and quality checked throughout the UK and this was decentralised to staff geographically who found the administration process a strain. A very long fishbone indeed (perhaps looking more like a centipede) is a sure sign that you need to re-frame the problem.

The initial solution was to rationalise the demonstration staff and to centralise them, but this proved to be of somewhat limited attractiveness and also very difficult to implement. Then a newly-appointed manager looked at the problem again, but without getting entangled in the existing problem diagnosis, and solved it with an entirely different strategy: outsourcing it!

A final point on fishbone analysis is that sometimes managers new to the technique feel that it is little more than a brainstorm. We are inclined to disagree. Whilst personally averse to much more structured fishbones and to structured diagnosis checklists, the fishbone does appear to perform a lot more than a loose brainstorm, and in particular it helps to:

- visualise the problem, and in such a way that it is more likely to lead to diagnosing other potential root causes;

- share that visualisation more powerfully than with a simple list of bullet points;

- generate sub-fishbones and thus network the web of causes;

- trace the apparent root cause back to the real root cause (a simple listing of 'causes' is more likely to lead to a mixture of symptoms and root causes).

Of all the techniques we teach, fishbone analysis is perhaps one of the most popular techniques. Whilst its original background was in TQM its possible application is much more diverse.

Before we move on next to Wishbone analysis, try this exercise.

EXERCISE – FISHBONE ANALYSIS

For one pharma project within your business which addresses a key organisational problem, ask yourself:

- What is the main symptom of the problem?
- What are its root causes? (Go back, if necessary, to the ultimate root causes using fishbone analysis – sub-fishbones)
- How might you dissolve or mitigate these problems, either for each of the bones or using a smaller, higher-level number of interventions?
- What project would now address this situation? Please define its objectives, scope and strategy.

Our final detailed diagnostic technique (to help us scope the pharm project) is Performance Driver analysis.

PERFORMANCE DRIVER ANALYSIS

Performance driver analysis is another way of performing business diagnosis as a means of diagnosing a pharma project, particularly one with a more direct operational impact (as opposed to it being more longer-term, R&D). This technique is highly complementary to fishbone analysis.

The technique is particularly useful for:

- business turnaround projects;

- diagnosing organisational issues and difficulties;

- defining problems to improve business performance generally.

The technique is as follows:

1. Identify the business or organisational area which is either the main focus of the pharma project or which may generate projects out of it.

2. Separate out the factors which are enabling the business or organisational unit to perform well (the key performance drivers). Draw them vertically as arrows (as per Figure 3.4) in proportion to their perceived relative strength.

3. Identify those factors which are holding performance back, or which are actually reducing performance (the performance brakes). Again, draw them in vertically in proportion to their perceived relative strength.

4. Step back from the picture and see whether, overall, the balance of performance drivers/brakes is strongly or weakly positive, is neutral or is actually negative.

Further areas to reflect on are:

- Are there linkages between the forces or patterns or underlying themes in them?

- To what extent are the key performance drivers external or internal?

- Do specific performance brakes warrant further diagnosis (possibly through fishbone analysis) in order to identify possible performance breakthrough projects?

- Or, might a single, well-focused project deal with many of these performance brakes with one hit?

- Might their possibly be one or more breakthrough or continuous improvement projects aimed at strengthening existing, minor performance drivers, or even introducing new ones?

The performance driver analysis can either be done by mixing internal and external performance drivers, or these may be separated out to form two discrete outputs. Interestingly, managers generally find this technique more powerful than conventional strengths and weakness and opportunities and threats (SWOT) analysis, as it deals more directly with the variables impacting on performance rather than, for instance, 'nice-to-have' strengths.

In Figure 3.4 we see a high growth bioscience business which is now facing the challenge of maintaining its flexibility and responsiveness even though its organisation and processes have grown far more complex.

This highlights (potentially) the need for breakthrough projects in:

- business process re-engineering;

- culture change and management development;

- project management and strategy prioritisation.

Performance driver analysis can also be used:

- to tease out deficiencies in organisational capability;

- to examine the strengths and weaknesses of a team before embarking on any team-building or management restructuring project;

- to assess staff at a micro-level who are underperforming, to establish a turnaround (or redeployment) plan for the project; anyone who has experienced having a member of their staff undergoing a disciplinary process will know what I mean about this being a 'project' – these situations are invariably complex, have a targeted result over a particular time, and are difficult and distracting.

Amplifying the second point above, one of our recent projects was to do some team-building for a clinical research department. The performance driver analysis highlighted a number of areas of undigested internal development, and greater organisational complexity, offset by staff enthusiasm and energy. This enabled the team to make internal adjustments, and to manage upwards more effectively. All of these initiatives were project managed, using the diagnostic techniques described in this chapter.

Once again, performance driver analysis can be supplemented with prioritisation techniques including: AID analysis (to identify which ones should then be focused on) and urgency–importance analysis (see Chapter 4).

EXERCISE – PERFORMANCE DRIVER ANALYSIS

Spend a few minutes thinking through an issue which might subsequently give rise to a business improvement project (for example a restructuring, process change or organisational development).

Identify one key business dilemma which you may wish to resolve and, possibly, through one or more pharma projects, and ask yourself:

- What are the key *external* performance drivers and brakes, and how important are these?
- What are the key *internal* performance drivers and brakes, and how important are these?
- Which of these drivers would you like to focus on as one or more business projects, and what might the scope of these be?

WISHBONE ANALYSIS

Wishbone analysis, although similar in shape superficially to fishbone analysis, is a quite different animal. Whilst fishbone analysis focuses on problems, wishbone analysis looks at opportunities. Not all pharma projects, by any means, are primarily responses to problems but are very much of an 'opportunity' nature. We therefore require a method of scoping out an opportunity.

With wishbone analysis we begin with some tentative vision. This is drawn at the left-hand side of the page to signify that this is our starting point. To the right-hand side of the picture, again as a series of bones, we draw out *all* the factors which need to line up in order to deliver the particular vision which we started off with.

These bones not only give us the *necessary* factors (or pre-conditions) for success, but also the *sufficient* conditions. Another way of thinking about the wishbone factors is that they are the prerequisites of fulfilling your project vision or goal.

To illustrate wishbone analysis let us take a look at the example of a successful clinical trial Figure 3.5 highlights not merely the more obvious pre-conditions of success but also some less than obvious factors, including:

- a 'cunning' way of ensuring just-in-time patient recruitment;

- a very experienced project manager who is not overloaded with other work;

- excellent training of project team members;

- no occurrences of individuals within the team being taken off to other projects;

- seasonal factors, like illness and holidays have been fully taken into account;

- excellent positioning and communication of the projects.

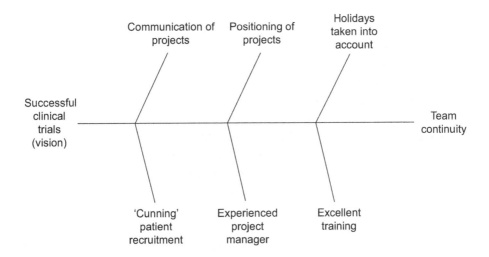

Figure 3.5   Wishbone analysis – success for clinical trials

The bones of the wishbone are not minor alignment areas, they are *major*. Indeed, where they are within the company's own domain of control then they are typically clever, innovative – if not downright *cunning*. Certainly they are not in any sense *average*.

This is a most important point and one which distinguishes wishbone analysis from other planning techniques and from a simple brainstorm. Wishbone thinking is very much an imaginative rather than a purely deductive activity.

Doing an effective wishbone certainly doesn't include linear thinking. Instead, think of it as being more of an imaginative spiral upwards: take an idea, explore around the idea, then take it up one level of cleverness. Leave it perhaps for a while, spiralling up other ideas and then come back to it to see if you can develop it further. Review the new levels of thinking, seeing what new linkages can be made between the various different clusters of ideas.

This creative process has much in common with the notion of 'helicopter thinking' which we explored in Chapter 1. This helicopter or spiral thinking can be done at multiple levels: at the project concept level itself (what are we trying to do anyway?), at the high-level factors of alignment, or even at a more micro level. Indeed, it is perfectly possible – and desirable – to do a mini-wishbone to support each and every bone of the wishbone. The various alignment factors (for the success of the pharma project) should also have at least some flavour of the 'cunning plan'.

As with fishbone analysis, it is a very sensible idea to perform this analysis on separate pages or flipcharts – to avoid clutter. And in the same way as with the fishbone, you will need to stress that there is no particular order or structure to the bones of the wishbone – just let the creative flow develop. Usually there will be at least some indirect linkage between one bone of the wishbone and the others. Nor is there any special significance to what alignment factor you put at the right-hand side or the end of the wishbone.

Wishbone analysis can also (in due course) be prioritised. Various methods of prioritisation can be applied using techniques which we develop later on in the book, particularly:

- AID analysis (Chapter 4): this helps identify how feasible doing it is likely to be given our domain of influence and control;

- urgency-importance analysis (Chapter 4): this helps to prioritise 'when we should do it and in which sequence';

- uncertainty-importance analysis (Chapter 4): this helps to evaluate the vulnerability of our wishbone strategy.

Clearly it would be over-the-top to use every single one of these techniques simultaneously on a pharma project at this phase. Nevertheless, it is quite possible that two of these processes will help and also that at a later stage you will find it useful to try three, or all four.

So, wishbone analysis is an imaginative way of any pharma project as an alignment system. This system of alignment may well incorporate:

- the factors both internal and external to the project;

- the factors which are both easily controlled, and less easy to control;

- the factors which are in the present and also factors which are in the future.

Besides being used to scope a project, wishbone analysis is also relevant to developing the project strategy in more depth (see Chapter 4 for other techniques), and finally it can also be used to monitor the project.

To practice wishbone analysis, try this next exercise.

EXERCISE – WISHBONE ANALYSIS

For one pharma project which you have sufficient knowledge of, ask yourself:

- What is your over-arching vision or goal?
- What factors need to line up to deliver that vision?
- Whether you have high or low influence over these?
- How attractive/difficult to implement is each one of the bones of your wishbone?

GAP ANALYSIS

A further diagnostic tool for project scoping is gap analysis – to help define the difference between where we are now and where we want to be in the future. Gap analysis is a classic planning technique (Ansoff, 1965) which is now relatively neglected by managers. As an approximation, and based on running countless public courses over the years, only about 10 per cent of managers have heard of gap analysis, and only perhaps 5 per cent have actually used it properly. Many major pharma companies, too, do not use gap analysis effectively, even though there do not seem to be any other alternative techniques for linking strategy development, business breakthroughs, business plans, and shareholder value creation.

CASE EXAMPLE – A PHARMACEUTICAL COMPANY PERFORMS A GAP ANALYSIS FOR THE FIRST TIME

Several years ago a major pharma company with much of its operations in Germany started to experiment with gap analysis on an important programme of business development products.

Initially, they resisted the idea of retaining a 'gap' in their plans – which they had not yet completed. They professed to sacrifice realism for the sake of avoiding the embarrassment of the residual gap.

They were only finally persuaded when their facilitator pointed out that all they needed to do was to flag up that a gap still existed, but that ongoing efforts in directions x, y and z were being made to complete the gap.

Figure 3.6 gives us a classic example of a gap analysis. The horizontal axis is time and the vertical axis is always one related to business performance – in this case profitability. The base line of the business is, in this case, one of decline – which is typically the norm under a 'do-nothing' plan, unless competitor conditions are actually relaxing.

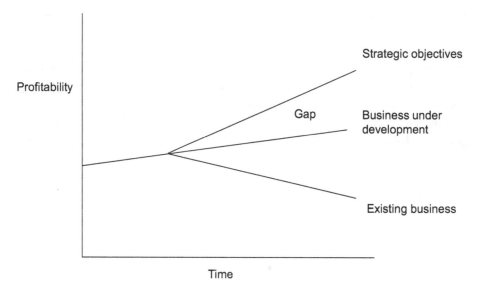

Figure 3.6   Strategic gap analysis

The planning line above reflects projects under development. It would be an accident if the base line of the business plus projects under development (whether breakthrough or simply continuous improvement) happened to deliver business objectives (the top line in Figure 3.6). These business objectives are frequently of a higher order of stretch, basically due either to:

- the requirements to deliver growth in shareholder value anyway; or

- the need to stretch managers' thinking about the art of the possible, making them more entrepreneurial and less bureaucratic in their style; or

- the tendency for top managers to see their jobs as being one of 'artificial stretch' – so that to get a particular quantum of extra performance you need always to ask for twice or even three times that quantum to get what you want.

Certainly, the first two reasons for gap analysis above (shareholder value and creative stretch) are laudable. The third area (artificial stretch) is more dubious. Although one cannot change how organisations actually want to behave (especially in a book!), it is worthwhile flagging the downsides of artificial stretch in gap analysis, especially in the pharma industry. These downsides include:

- Senior managers in pharma companies taking stretch goals at face value, then trying to achieve them by trying to force the pace and, by squeezing the results out of them, resulting in energy burn-out, a loss of commitment and enthusiasm. This has particularly been observed by one of the authors in clinical research projects.

- Projects being taken on with stretch goals, but which are doomed to delay or failure because of insufficient resources.

- The unreality of project goals causes a cerebral disconnection in pharma managers. Because they have been asked to do 'mission impossible' they never even get off the cerebral starting line of thinking, step-by-step, how they are going to get there and with what 'cunning plan' or strategy.

- The organisation as a whole may have taken on too many projects generally. Many pharma companies have a large number of drugs in development making it difficult for organisation to be able to resource appropriately. Top managers themselves know in their heart of hearts that there is going to be strategic slippage (or 'strategic droop' – Grundy, 1998) across the piece. So, they start too many projects in the hope that this will compensate for disappointing results. This culminates in harmful inter-project rivalry, excess competition for resources, unhelpful politics and sometimes a performance inferior to that from doing even *half* that number of pharma projects.

Primitive gap analysis can therefore be most unhelpful, causing strategic panic in the organisation as managers take on impossible or unrealistic challenges. Unless gap analysis is supplemented with solid, strategic thinking, especially on *how* the project will be delivered with competitive advantage, then gap analysis is unlikely to be resilient.

Having made these caveats clear, gap analysis – provided that it is well supported by imaginative strategic thinking and by well-resourced implementation plans – is an essential technique. Gap analysis can highlight both the need for a specific pharma project and also give some idea of the scope of its outputs, and also what is needed to be delivered, and by when.

As gap analysis essentially focuses on the future, it does give a reference point to begin working backwards from, for unless one has some framework for where one wants/needs to be – and by when – the project may well be underscoped and underpositioned.

Now we suggest that you try the next exercise.

EXERCISE – GAP ANALYSIS

For one area of business performance, organisational change or operational improvement in your pharma company, ask yourself:

- What is our current strategic position, operational performance or level of organisational capability?

- If we do nothing (or do relatively little) where will it be in, say, one, two or three years' time?
- What existing projects or ongoing processes will mitigate any decline in position, performance or capability?
- Where do we really need/want to be in this area – again in one, two or three years' time (strategic objectives)?
- What other options (other than this specific project) might close the gap?
- What is the gap between the likely position without any new pharma project and our strategic objectives?
- How will our project contribute to filling this gap, and will actioning it be both necessary *and* sufficient to bridge that gap?

The above exercise should generate much rich thinking, particularly about:

- Where are we now? This is frequently far from self evident, and may require some more detailed analysis and research to establish the base position.

- What is the likely deterioration in position with a 'do nothing' strategy? Here we need to evaluate the external pressures for change very thoroughly. Whilst procrastination is not always a good policy, it may be possible to delay the project somewhat so that we are able to focus on fewer breakthrough pharma projects at any one time. This, in turn, might allow us to perform a more effective implementation of this project when its time comes around. A critical part of the assessment here is that of the cost and risk of delay.

- Are the objectives of the project realistic and reasonable – given the nature of the pharma industry and the conditions under which we are therefore developing projects?

- Is there a better way (considering other options) of closing the pharma gap?

Gap analysis can be applied to:

- targeting the project's end-results;

- revenue gaps;

- cost gaps;

- time-to-market gaps;

- capability gaps.

To do a more extensive gap analysis we can use the 'from- to' (sometimes called FT) analysis below.

FROM–TO ANALYSIS

From–to analysis (see Figure 3.7 for a generic example) is another useful tool for scoping projects, especially for organisational change or for operational improvement. Where a development project has a significant impact on 'how we do things around here' or the 'paradigm' (see Johnson and Scholes, 1992; Grundy, 1993b) – a concept used by SmithKline Beecham (now GSK) during its culture change programme, then it is essential that at least a rudimentary from–to analysis is conducted.

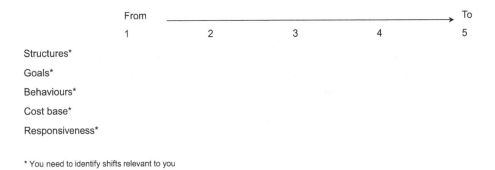

Figure 3.7   Using 'from–to' analysis

The 'paradigm' embraces a raft of organisational processes, some of which are 'hard' and tangible and some of which are 'soft' and intangible.

For example, managers within one major pharma company used a from–to analysis based specifically on the paradigm to scope their organisational change project. This helped them to get their minds around the 'soft' as well as the 'hard' factors, as follows.

Paradigm	From	To
Power	Restricted	Resides at the lowest appropriate level
Structure	Hierarchical	Flatter
Controls	Instinctive and 'by seat of pants'	Measured objectives
Routines	Retrospective looking	Live and forward looking
Rituals	Loose plans	Structured plans
Myths	The 'Mighty Pharma Corporation'	Real world
Stories	Our job well done	Delighted customers
Symbols	Status hierarchy	Rewards for performance
Management style	Aloof	Open

This kind of analysis can also be used to monitor the progress of a project, perhaps using a score of 1 to 5 with 1 being the 'from' and possible 5 being the 'to'. (In some situations, however, we might well be starting off with better than 1, as we might already have made some progress towards our goals, prior to embarking on the project. Equally, we might wish to go all out for a 5, as a 4 or even 3 score might be more realistic and acceptable, depending upon the situation.)

The above example of from–to analysis is very much a more 'gourmet' approach. We see a semi-structured approach being used to generate the key shifts which the pharma project is aimed at delivering. A simplified approach is to quickly brainstorm the 'froms' and 'tos' in a way much more specific to a particular project. Our main caveat here is that you *really must* think about the softer factors which are needed to shift, for example, behaviours, attitudes and mind-set generally.

To perform a from–to analysis you need to carry out the following steps:

• What are you trying to shift (the critical categories)?

• By how much are you trying to shift them (the horizontal from–to shifts)?

By now it may have become apparent to you that from–to analysis is essentially an extended form of gap analysis (see our previous section). Because it breaks the gap down into a number of dimensions, it is generally more specific than gap analysis, and is frequently the next step on.

EXERCISE – FROM–TO ANALYSIS

For one pharma project of your choice and in particular one for which there is already an existing state of affairs which you are trying to change or shift, ask yourself:

- What are the key dimensions which you are trying to shift?
- What are the extremes of these shifts (from left to right), that is, where have you started from originally, and where would you like to end up ultimately?
- Where you are actually now? (Note, this does not have to be a 1.)
- Where do you want to be as a result of this project? (Note: this does not have to be a 5.)
- What specific actions or interventions might make each shift feasible?

In our final question above we stray into project strategy – indeed, like wishbone analysis, from–to analysis can be a useful means of developing project strategy, besides also scoping the project.

A common confusion which is well worth addressing at this point is about which tool to use and when. Managers are often unsure whether you use wishbone analysis or from–to analysis in scoping their project.

First, and quite simply, do not attempt to use from–to analysis for an entirely new situation. For example, if you are launching a new drug, setting up a new R&D centre or penetrating a new pharma distribution channel, you will not have a 'from'. In this situation, just use wishbone analysis.

Only where you feel it is worthwhile reflecting upon your existing competencies before you do something quite new is it worthwhile doing a from–to analysis.

Where you have an existing situation, a number of choices exist:

- Do a from–to analysis (as above).

- Where the future is more important than the legacy, go direct to wishbone analysis.

- Where you are not very clear about where you are now, why you are there, and what might have gone wrong in the past:

    - begin with a fishbone analysis;
    - then, either move onto a wishbone analysis (to develop the future vision and factors of alignment); or
    - move from the fishbone analysis directly into the 'from–to'.

The above tools are highly flexible and providing you are following a logic and the techniques do seem to fit with and be coping well with the context, then just follow their natural flow.

A good rule of thumb is to think for a few minutes – before you actually use any technique:

If I use this technique or this logic, what is likely to come out?

Use this as a reality test before committing time to analysis,. By doing this, around 90 per cent of moments of frustration will be avoided.

Identifying the Project's Key Objectives

Now we have thoroughly diagnosed the context for the pharma project using a selection of project diagnosis tools, we can now set the project's key objectives with greater clarity. Whilst this may seem to be an obvious and self-evident part of the process, it is often not. There may be several dimensions of the project's objectives, including its:

- strategic objectives;

- operational objectives;

- organisational objectives;

- financial objectives.

For instance, strategic objectives might include:

- penetrating a new drug market to gain a certain percentage of market share;

- gaining a particular competitive position within a geographic market for a drug;

- creating new opportunities for strategy development – through developing R&D competencies, for example;

- generating tangible synergies or spin-offs in other areas of the business.

Operational objectives – for their part – might include:

- improving efficiency levels – for example within clinical trials;

- resolving performance difficulties or bottlenecks – for example in distribution or IT;

- simplifying operational processes;

- achieving world-class operational standards;

- achieving very high service standards, or zero defects in pharma manufacture;

- developing new processes, for example, implementing electronic data capture (EDC – to collect clinical trial data instead of using traditional paper documentation).

Organisational objectives might include:

- building existing competencies;

- creating entirely new competencies;

- improved team-working (for example, cross culturally);

- increasing organisational responsiveness and flexibility;

- simplifying the organisation;

- creating specific behaviours – for example, leadership or creativity;

- shifting the organisational mind-set;

- making it a genuinely international organisation – critical for global drug development.

Financial objectives might include:

- improved rate of return on assets;

- improved return on sales, or on margins;

- reduced overhead costs;

- payback over a particular period (for an investment) (that is, how long do you take to get your outlay back);

- net present value (the economic value of the future volume of net cash flows less investment).

Whilst every pharma project will have its core objectives (which will almost certainly be multiple), there will almost certainly be some secondary objectives too. Although a sub-set of these objectives may be reasonably self-evident, there may still be some ambiguity about what the pharma project is actually about. It is therefore imperative to define the primary *and* the secondary objectives explicitly rather than leave them to the risks of mis-communication and misunderstanding throughout the organisation.

CASE EXAMPLE – DEVELOPING A CORPORATE PLAN

For example, taking the key objectives of a hypothetical project to develop a corporate plan for a major pharma company – which has been growing very rapidly, and now needs to set better priorities – as a basis then for managing the drug portfolio, and operational and organisational development, we see the following:

Strategic objectives:

- to define the strategic position of the group and of its individual divisions;
- to identify and diagnose the key strategic issues at both the divisional and corporate levels;
- to define and prioritise a number of areas for strategic breakthrough and to evaluate the key strategic options facing divisions and the group;
- to help us to manage our external stakeholders more effectively, particularly institutional and major private holders of shares.

Operational objectives:

- to provide a better framework for operational decision-making – especially at the drug programme level.

Organisational objectives:

- to help define key skills gaps (present and future) as input to organisational development – both for technical and management skills;
- to help us re-examine our mind-set of 'who we are, what are we here to do, and how?' – including definition of mission and values;
- to build strategic-thinking capability at business, divisional and corporate levels;
- to allow high-potential managers to participate in the debate about the future of the pharma group and of the business units within it, both to develop them for the future, and to enthuse them.

Financial objectives:

- to provide a framework for strategic financial management of the group;

- to provide input to the strategic and financial three-year plan;
- to estimate investment requirements;
- to help prioritise investment – organically in alliances and in organic development.

This is quite a long list but by making these objectives explicit we can later go back and ask the question:

To what extent did the pharma project meet, or not meet, its key objectives, and if it fell short, why?

What is notable about the above example is that the strategic review had a number of 'softer' or organisational objectives. Arguably, if these had been met they might have, in the longer-term, equal or more impact than delivering a formal strategic plan which would, over time, be somewhat less relevant.

EXERCISE – DEFINING YOUR PHARMACEUTICAL PROJECT'S KEY OBJECTIVES

What are the current objectives of one pharma project which you are currently dealing with? How do these objectives cover the following different types:

- Strategic objectives?
- Financial objectives?
- Operational objectives?
- Organisational objectives?

Did breaking down these objectives in more detail help you to really think about the full rationale for doing the project?

Having established greater clarity on project objectives it is then worthwhile to go back to our earlier diagnosis, whether this was achieved using fishbone, wishbone, from–to or performance driver analysis. At this earlier stage the probable scope of the pharma project should have begun to emerge, potentially in the shape of an embryonic strategy. This scope can then be tested against the project's objectives, for example, to address these questions:

- Will achievement of the objectives deal fully or only partly with the problems or potential opportunity unearthed in the diagnosis phase?

- Are the objectives sufficiently complete to achieve this?

- Are the objectives becoming so complex that we may well need to think of splitting the project into separate projects, or at least into sub-projects?

The clearer the project's objectives are, the easier it is to interrelate the project to other projects, and also to begin to compile a business case for the project. It also becomes easier to decide on the most appropriate project management skills that are required. Also, control measures can be more readily derived. Finally, it becomes much easier to communicate the project and to position it with key stakeholders.

Resourcing the Project – to CRO or not to CRO?

Once we have set the objectives, it is important to start thinking about resources. With clinical research projects in particular there is invariably the decision as to whether to in-source or to out-source to a CRO (Contract Research Organisation).

CROs are playing a significant role in the pharma industry and particularly in clinical research. There are now more than 450 major CROs in Europe and the US, many offering a comprehensive range of services. In addition, there are many hundreds of small CROs with fewer than 50 staff. The variety is enormous, from freelance consultants, small one-office CROs to consortia of several national or international global CROs.

Some CROs are now the size of some of the less huge pharma companies. To achieve this growth they have hired more staff and often implemented the latest project management and technological systems. Using them wisely can therefore give you a project management edge. Like the pharma industry, the CRO situation is continually changing. Several small and/or inexperienced CROs have become insolvent and mergers and acquisitions are common.

The role of CROs in clinical research has expanded considerably in the past decade. CRO usage by the pharma industry has increased considerably, particularly for clinical research such as phase III studies. Also, sponsors are contracting out a broader range of pharma research activities to CROs and so the larger CROs now offer comprehensive preclinical and clinical development services. Such services may include:

- setting up and monitoring Phase I to IV clinical studies;

- statistics and data management;

- medical writing;

- safety monitoring and/or reporting;

- quality assurance;

- health economics;

- regulatory support;

- manufacturing;

- packaging and labelling clinical drug supplies;

- preclinical development;

- running phase I studies;

- central laboratory service;

- marketing (some CROs will provide this).

Monitoring clinical trials is one of the main areas where CROs provide a service to the pharma industry.

As the need to use CROs has increased dramatically during the past 15 years, sponsors are developing more comprehensive selection methods to help ensure that the CRO selected will meet the required criteria including carrying out their responsibilities to meet GCP. Many pharma companies have specific personnel responsible for selecting and managing CROs. Three criteria have been suggested for choosing a CRO: capability, compatibility and cost. Various checklists exist for selecting CROs, although several are available only within companies. The checklist below outlines the key considerations when selecting CROs:

1.   Obtain internal authorisation to select the CRO and estimate the budget needed. (Having some idea about how much the project will cost will help when evaluating the quotations from the CROs.)

2.   Draw up a list of CROs from which to obtain quotations. Sources of information include:

   - CRO registers (for example, Technomark register, the CRO Capability Assessment Service (CROCAS) database, the Pharmaceutical Contract Support Organisation register (PCSO);

   - consultants specialising in CRO evaluation;

   - personal recommendation;

   - company databases;

   - promotional literature and advertisements;

   - professional and scientific exhibitions.

3.   Prepare a confidentiality agreement, signed by each CRO approached.

4.   Prepare a request for proposal. This should include a list of all the activities required by the project and includes tasks that will be performed in-house and those to be contracted out. Activities that involve both parties should be listed under both headings. The CRO should be asked to quote against this list of items (see Table 3.1 for an example). Milestones and a timeline, as well as background information about the project including a study summary should be provided. Other information such as a protocol (the document which describes the procedure needed to carry out a particular clinical study) and CRF (or Case Report Form, which is a document to record all the protocol required information on each trial subject),

if available, may also be useful to the CROs. The CROs should be given instructions for preparing a bid. In addition to the quotation the CRO should be asked to provide the following:

- a description of how its range of services would relate to the activities requested by the sponsor;

- details of its experience in the therapeutic area;

- curricula vitae and training records for personnel who would be likely to carry out the key activities on the project;

- an estimate of the number of personnel who would be expected to be working on the project;

- whether any aspects of the project will be subcontracted;

- procedures and practices: standard operating procedures (SOPs) should be available for the sponsor to review so that the CRO's ability to comply with good clinical practice (GCP) can be assessed. It may also be useful to assess comparability with the sponsor's SOPs;

- details of quality assurance;

- information about the company's history, size, organisational and financial stability.

The CROs should also be asked to recommend alternative strategies to the proposal. All the CROs should be given the same information. The sponsor should ensure the terms of agreement and schedule of payments are acceptable to the CROs. A deadline for receipt of the bid should be given.

5. Short-listed candidates should be invited to present their proposals to the sponsor.

6. The sponsor should carry out a site evaluation of the short-listed CROs.

7. To evaluate the bids, sponsor personnel involved in evaluating the CROs (this may be a team or an individual) should use a standard rating sheet to assess the CRO's technical and organisational capabilities.

8.   To help ensure the CROs are able to comply with GCP it is advisable for the sponsor to audit the CRO before the final selection is made. Sponsors frequently audit two short-listed CROs.

Once the CRO has been selected a thorough agreement between the parties should be drawn up. This must include the division of responsibilities. Contracts usually contain a set of general terms and conditions. This usually covers payments, timeframes, service standards, any penalty clauses or bonus payments, confidentiality provisions, details of the procedure to follow if either side terminates the contract, project budget, payment schedule and a list of the work to be carried out.

Preparing the detailed request for proposal is worthwhile to ensure that the CROs and the sponsor are clear what their responsibilities are, and because it will ensure that bids are compatible. Following the above procedure will help select the most suitable CRO and help lay the foundation for the study.

The selection of CROs is a time-consuming and intensive procedure. As the market has matured it may not always be necessary to go through this lengthy procedure to select a CRO for each project; instead sponsors are commonly establishing strategic alliances with CROs. The CROs are entering relationships with sponsors where they offer preferential pricing for being a preferred provider.

Table 3.1   Request for proposal: responsibilities for study services

RESPONSIBILITIES		
Activity	Sponsor	CRO
1. Study materials		
Write protocol		
Process ethical approval		
Design CRFs		
Print CRFs		
Supply study drug(s)		
Supply comparative drugs		
Package clinical supplies		
Label clinical supplies		
Ship study materials		
Prepare randomisation codes		

RESPONSIBILITIES		
Activity	**Sponsor**	**CRO**
2. Study set-up		
Identify study sites		
Evaluate study sites		
Negotiate investigator fee		
Select investigators		
Conduct investigator meeting		
Train site personnel		
Obtain ethical approval		
Collect pre-study documents		
Conduct initiation visit		
3. Study conduct		
Monitor sites every X weeks		
Verify X % of CRFs		
Telephone sites every X weeks		
Provide monitoring reports		
Provide status reports every X weeks		
Handle safety reporting		
4. Study Close		
Perform drug accountability		
Dispose of unused supplies		
Document corrections to CRFs		
Conduct GCP audits		
5. Data management		
Design database		
Clean up CRFs		
Enter CRFs into database		
Verify data		
Code data using X dictionary		
Provide interim analysis report		
Perform quality control on data		
Perform statistical analysis		
Prepare clinical study report according to ICH GCP requirements		
6. Other (study specific responsibilities)		

Insert ✓ against appropriate item in the table to indicate whose responsibility the task is.

Source: Derived from R. Vogel and N. Schober. *Achieving Results with CROs: Requesting and Evaluating Proposals from CROs*. Derived from Vogel and Schober. Good Clinical Practice 1997, Scrip Reports, BS 862, 111-112.

In conclusion, CROs are playing more active and broader roles in clinical research and drug development in general. A few of the largest CROs are now working in partnership with some pharma companies to share the risk of drug development, with the aim of sharing in the profits, which can be substantially higher than the margins on normal CRO services.

To improve project management with CROs some companies have recently introduced agreements where CROs will share the costs of overspend with the sponsor company. This has encouraged CROs to discuss problems early on with the sponsor and has frequently enabled a solution to be found that resolves the issues and avoids the need to overspend the budget.

Where studies are contracted out to CROs, the success of the project will greatly depend on how the CRO carries out the work, as well as the control the sponsor retains over the project. Therefore, it is essential that the sponsor takes great care in evaluating and choosing which CRO(s) to work with. (We will be taking a brief look at a technique for evaluating CRO's later in the Project Option Grid (Figure 4.2)).

Having now covered the project's objectives and some of the resourcing issues we can now move onto positioning the project, and particularly to think about its key stakeholders.

Identifying the Project's Key Stakeholders – and its Difficulty

Whille there is a more detailed account of stakeholder analysis in Chapter 4, it is necessary to touch on stakeholders briefly. First, a stakeholder can be defined as 'an individual or a group of individuals with an influence over the pharma project' through being one of the following:

- a decision-maker;

- an adviser on the decision;

- a user or victim of the project, either during implementation or on project completion.

Clearly a particular stakeholder might fall into two or even three of these categories. For example, a decision-maker may be involved in implementation, and also as a potential user. Or, an implementer might also ultimately be a user. Overlaps like this are often helpful as, otherwise, the decision-making can become dislocated from the implementation reality.

Stakeholders can be either internal or external to the organisation (like a regulatory authority or ethical committee). While external stakeholders frequently *are* important, it is often the internal stakeholders that are the really crucial players. Therefore it is to the internal stakeholders our attention most frequently turns.

At the project definition stage, the *minimum* we should do is to identify the likely stakeholders for the pharma project. This can be done by preparing a very simple stakeholder periscope picture as follows:

1. Draw three concentric circles on a flipchart with the centre containing core players, the second circle containing secondary players, and the third circle containing peripheral players.

2. Place Post-it® notes of key players according to whether they are likely to fall into the three categories.

3. Within each circle place stakeholders most likely to be on board at the top with those less likely to be on board at the bottom. Those we are unclear about will be placed in the middle.

Figure 3.8 gives a quick illustration.

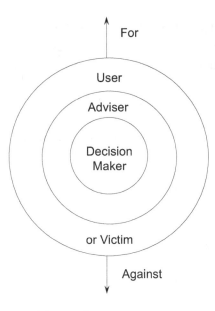

Figure 3.8   The stakeholder periscope

This figure does not discriminate between the levels of influence of primary and secondary players (for that see Chapter 6), nor does it dig deeper down into their agendas. Nevertheless, it gives a good first cut of where stakeholders might be located, at least in sufficient detail to help identify to whom the project needs to be communicated.

EXERCISE – USING THE STAKEHOLDER PERISCOPE

For a pharma project of your choice, and using the stakeholder periscope picture, ask yourself:

- Who are the primary stakeholders?
- Who are the secondary stakeholders?
- Who are the peripheral stakeholders?
- For each of these, are they likely to be for, in neutral, or against the project?
- Are any of the stakeholders likely to shift over time, either (a) from one category of stakeholder to another, or (b) from positive attitude to negative, or vice versa?

Having identified the pharma project's objectives and the likely stakeholders, it is now possible to define a most appropriate communication message and strategy. If this is done effectively there will be a number of benefits:

- the project will be better understood, and misunderstandings avoided;

- opinion should be pre-mobilised in the project's favour;

- objections (or reservations about) the project will be surfaced and can be dealt with;

- implementation issues might also be revealed.

The above will have a big influence now over the difficulty of the project, as it changes over time.

Nevertheless, at minimum we should think about:

- What are the key phases of the pharma project?

- During which phases will we encounter the most/least difficulty?

- Why?

As a quick-and-dirty technique for identifying possible difficulty ahead you can, hold the technique of fishbone analysis in your mind whilst you try to sense the future (to identify *why* it might be difficult at different phases).

EXERCISE – ANTICIPATING IMPLEMENTATION DIFFICULTY

For a new pharma project:

- What are the most probable sources of its likely difficulty? (Use fishbone analysis.)
- Have you done similar projects in the past, and what have the difficulties been? Are these likely to add to the difficulties you have identified above? (If so, extend your fishbone.)

> • Where you have had little experience of projects like this in the past, might this lack of experience in itself generate difficulties? (Again, if so, add to your fishbone.)

Conclusion

Project diagnosis is a crucial phase in more contemporary pharma project management. If sufficient time and thought is spent at this phase there is every chance that we will be doing the right (as opposed to the wrong) project, and that we will have fully understood its scope.

The diagnosis techniques for the current position, together with objectives setting and preliminary thinking about stakeholders and implementation difficulty, should stand us in good stead for our next phase: developing project strategy and plans.

RECOMMENDATION

We hope you have spent time doing the exercises in the first three chapters. If not, we would recommend completing them now, as this will increase the value you get from the remainder of this book.

4

Developing Pharmaceutical Project Strategy and Plans

Introduction

In this chapter we look more specifically at pharma project options and their initial prioritisation at a strategic level, using the 'project option grid'. The project option grid has proved to be extremely popular with the companies which we have worked with and is perceived as adding value to the development of a more contemporary project management process. We also examine different options for implementing them, for example with 'push' versus 'pull' strategies.

Our next major phase involves a more detailed exploration of methods for prioritising different pharma projects which compete against each other at a more operational level using AID analysis. In order to explore their difficulty in more depth, we look at force-field analysis and the supporting stakeholder analysis techniques.

Once the project strategy has become clearer we are able to move into much more detailed project planning and programming. The key activities of the project are scoped using 'how–how' analysis. We are then able to plot activities over time using classic Gantt chart analysis. We examine the project's critical path through mapping which projects are interdependent with others, and identify the order in which these need to be implemented.

We then touch on uncertainty analysis using the uncertainty grid to test out the likely robustness of implementation. This helps us to check out and adjust, if necessary, the project's critical path. This process is supported using importance-influence analysis to target the factors which we can do most about. These techniques are increasingly important in the pharma industry which is becoming increasingly less and less predictable.

In the chapter's final section we look at more tailored approaches to using project management software within the pharma industry.

Developing Project Options and Strategies

Whilst it is perfectly possible to evaluate a number of project options in one's head, the task becomes increasingly difficult as the number of project options increase, and as more than three major criteria need to be considered. This moves from 'very difficult' to 'mission impossible' when working with a team of managers, especially ones with strong egos and strong views about most areas of strategy and pharma projects generally.

Some more formal way of prioritising strategic options needs to be found and this is manifest in the project option grid (see Figure 4.1) which looks at a number of options against the following generic criteria:

Strategic attractiveness:	This depends upon the strength of growth in demand and competitive pressure (in a particular drug market), and also upon existing and potential future competitive position vis-à-vis other drugs/therapeutic treatments. Or it depends on the extent to which the project positions the pharma company advantageously for future opportunity.
Financial attractiveness:	This is determined by the value and cost drivers underpinning it, and the relative investment at stake.
Implementation difficulty:	This is the cumulative difficulty over the life-cycle of the project.
Uncertainty and risk:	These are the fundamental assumptions upon which the project is founded and their degree of sensitivity to external and internal shock.
Acceptability to stakeholders:	This is the level of existing and (probable) future support for the project, given the agendas and influence of the key players with an impact on it.

Options / Criteria	Option 1	Option 2	Option 3	Option 4
Strategic attractiveness				
Financial attractiveness*				
Implementation difficulty				
Uncertainty and risk				
Acceptability (to stakeholders)				

* Benefits less costs, net cash flows relative to investment

Figure 4.1   Project option grid

The Project option grid is completed first by discussion within the decision-making team prior to defining any further detailed investigations required to collect more data. Even at this stage, creative options can be identified (see the various columns – Option 1, Option 2, Option 3, and so on). This may be used for mutually exclusive options, for example drug number one, two or three, or for different ways of developing the drug, or clinically testing the drug (for example through doing it in-house or by using a CRO).

Each of these project options is then evaluated either as:

✓✓✓ very attractive

✓✓   fairly attractive

✓   not attractive

(Remember that 'very difficult' and 'very uncertain' will count as one tick.)

The project option grid thus leads to a much more focused, well-informed discussion relative to that which occurs normally.

For example, in the project option grid in Figure 4.2, two options for *implementing* a clinical trial are examined, one without a CRO and one with one (this is based on a real specific example. Therefore the conclusion from the analysis will depend on the specific CRO used and the specific sponsor. It will not necessarily be the case that using a CRO is always a less attractive option. It was just the case for the specific example given). The 'without CRO' option is more strategically and financially attractive, but is perceived to be more difficult and potentially uncertain. However, on balance, the stakeholders rate this as 'highly attractive'.

	Do it yourself	With CRO
Strategic attractiveness	✓✓✓	✓✓
Financial attractiveness	✓✓✓	✓✓
Implementation difficulty	✓	✓✓
Uncertainty and risk	✓✓	✓✓
Stakeholder acceptability	✓✓✓	✓✓
Total score	12	10

Figure 4.2   Project option grid – using a CRO

On the other hand, the CROoption has much lower perceived difficultly and is of slightly less uncertainty, but it fails on strategic attractiveness and doesn't do too well on stakeholder acceptability. (Obviously, you have to define what you mean by 'strategic attractiveness' on a case-by-case basis.) Equally, we might have used the project option grid to appraise different CROs (with some additional criteria, such as financial strength, past reputation, particular clinical skills strengths and so on).

Key strategic questions to ask yourself about each project option are therefore as follows:

Strategic attractiveness:

- What are the key growth drivers (the factors causing the market to grow) impacting on your drug?

- How are these likely to change in future?

- What is the overall level of competitive pressure in this particular drug market (consider threat from new drugs under development by competitors or rivals, substitute therapies)?

- How might this change in the future?

- What is the relative competitive position of a therapy (for example in terms of likely therapeutic efficacy relative to cost of treatment)?

- How can we innovate to shift the attractiveness of the market (for example, a Viagra equivalent for women)?

Financial attractiveness

- What are the key value-creating activities which the project might generate and which add most/least value?

- How do these activities interact with one another?

- What are the key value and cost drivers within these activities? (Value drivers are those things either inside or outside of the business that either directly or indirectly generate cash; cost drivers are those same things which produce cash outflows.)

Implementation difficulty

- How inherently difficult is the pharma project to implement over time?

- Do we have *all* the key competencies to implement it?

- Is this the kind of pharma project *we naturally do well*?

Uncertainty and risk

- What are the key external uncertainties and risks?

- What are the key internal uncertainties and risks?

- How might some uncertainty/risk factors compound with others to undermine the project and impact on shareholder value?

Acceptability to stakeholders

- Who are the key stakeholders with an influence over (a) the project decision, and (b) its implementation and what are their agendas? (For example, the medics, the regulatory department and so on.)

- Given this, does the project have sufficient commitment to succeed?

Another way of representing these criteria more specifically for pharma project appraisal, and especially for portfolio analysis, is to disaggregate the economic criteria ('strategic' and financial') from the feasibility criteria.

EXERCISE – THE PROJECT OPTION GRID

For a pharma project of your choice, ask yourself:

- What are the key options (either for which project you will do, or for how you will do the project)?
- How attractive do these score on the project option grid?
- Could any of the options be revised to perhaps yield a higher attractiveness?

Whilst there are typically quite a number of options for *what* you might do, typically there are *even more* options for *how* you might do this.

The variations on implementation can include for instance:

- the timing of implementation;

- the duration of implementation;

- the phases of implementation;

- who to involve, and when;

- the amount of resources generally;

- the positioning of the project;

- whether to rely exclusively on external resources or whether to contract out (either in part or in whole);

- the *style* of implementation.

The final point on style of implementation brings us to the possibility of either a 'push' strategy or a 'pull' strategy, or perhaps a mix of both. A 'push' strategy is one where a number of key stakeholders are not involved in formulation of the project strategy. A 'pull' strategy is where all stakeholders are involved in the project strategy – to maximise their buy-in.

In a 'push' strategy there is a very strong organisational imperative to deliver a particular project result and also in its manner of delivery. In a 'pull' strategy there is much less – if any – sense of coercion. Here the project strategy is seen as being arrived at by as much consensus as possible, with enthusiasm being generated from within the ranks of the stakeholders upon which the change (or the project) impacts.

Both 'push' and 'pull' strategies derive from change theory. In change theory the style of implementation is prescribed differently, depending upon the situation (this being called a 'contingency approach'). Generally speaking, however, most pharma projects can and should incorporate a mix of *both* push and pull elements. For example, even in clinical trials projects which need to be driven very much 'top-down' in the organisation we can still get the project team to think about a different implementation option and to challenge the best balance between its intended results, time and costs. It is perfectly possible (and desirable), for example, to have a project objective laid down fundamentally as a push strategy, whilst the means of the implementation is left more open – as a 'pull' strategy.

Also, one may well need to use a different mix of pull versus push strategies during different phases of the pharma project. At an early stage of a project aiming at effecting organisational change within a pharma company, for example, one might seek input to future style, skills, and so on, at a participative level (through a 'pull' strategy). Next, one might communicate the overall future shape of the pharma company organisation as, more or less, a given (or as a 'push' strategy). Finally, one might run workshops with staff in their new positions to get them to think about how the new organisation can work best (shifting to a 'pull' strategy once more).

Having examined a powerful, if sophisticated way of prioritising pharma projects at a macro level, let us now look at more micro-level project prioritisation.

Attractiveness–Implementation Difficulty Analysis

By looking at a pharma project's relative attractiveness and its implementation difficulty one can now begin to evaluate projects at a micro level, and from a number of perspectives:

- one can prioritise a portfolio of projects, any one of which can be undertaken; or

- mutually exclusive projects can be prioritised;

- different options for implementing the same project concept can be evaluated; or

- the different parts or activities within a project can be prioritised.

The AID analysis grid subsumes both 'strategic' and 'financial' attractiveness into the vertical dimension of 'attractiveness' (the vertical axis). Together, these two criteria are effectively the equivalent to the idea of 'economic attractiveness' which we can see in Figure 4.3. Implementation difficulty and stakeholder acceptability are combined in the horizontal axis of implementation difficulty. (AID analysis (see Figure 4.4) was first developed through prioritisation of cost breakthroughs of Amersham plc some years ago, and is now in use as the standard technique for prioritisation in a number of other pharma companies.) 'Feasibility' analysis (which is virtually synonymous with implementation difficulty) is represented in Figure 4.5.

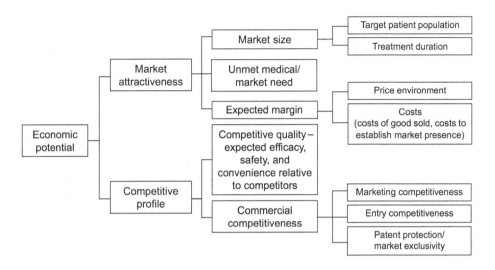

Figure 4.3   Economic criteria

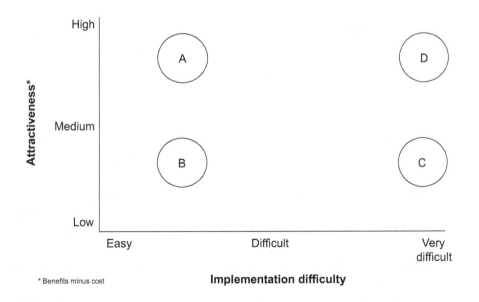

Figure 4.4   AID analysis

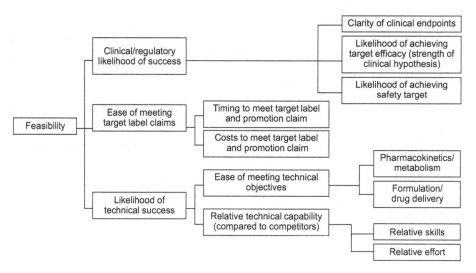

Figure 4.5   Feasibility criteria

AID analysis can thus be used as a portfolio technique for all projects, particularly those involving drug development.

Beginning with the vertical dimension of attractiveness one can now expand on the final bullet point above.

Only uncertainty (as a project option grid criterion) omitted completely from the AID grid – so we have a much simpler prioritisation area but one that does however omit uncertainty.

The project option grid and AID analysis are not mutually exclusive. The project option grid can be used first to evaluate different strategic options (either for different projects or for different ways of doing a specific project). Then the AID analysis might evaluate and prioritise sub-parts.

In some areas the sub-parts of a project may all have similar attractiveness. Where these are an absolutely essential part say, of a clinical trial, they all have to be done, so will be a on the horizontal line of from low to high difficulty.

It is sometimes the case that some parts of a project can be undertaken without doing others. For example, buying a pharma business is a project but the constituent parts of the business can be regarded as sub-projects to be retained or possibly disposed of.

Even where a project does consist of a number of sub-parts, which are not discretionary (such as a training programme), it is still possible usually to display their individual positionings on the AID grid. Without doubt some parts of the training will be more difficult to implement than others – and will thus have different positionings horizontally on the AID grid.

Thinking now about the vertical dimension of attractiveness, each part of a pharma restructuring project in a pharma company may vary in its relative benefits, and in its relative cost. For example, a restructuring project might have the following profile:

	Benefits (B)	Costs (C)	Attractiveness (B)-(C)
Pre-diagnosis	High	Medium	Medium
Pre-work	Low	Low	Low
Main programme	High	Medium	High/Medium
Interim support	Medium	Low	Medium
Follow-up programme	High	Low	High
Ongoing support	High	Low	High

The attractiveness-implementation tool (AID grid) enables trade-offs to be achieved between projects. The vertical dimension of the picture focuses on benefits minus costs. The horizontal dimension represents the total difficulty over time. This time is the time up until delivery of results, and not of completion of earlier project phases. This tool enables a portfolio of possible pharma projects to be prioritised. Figure 4.4 illustrates a hypothetical case.

Project A is seen as being both very attractive and relatively easy to implement. This project is non-contentious and will probably be given the go-ahead. Project C is relatively easy to decide upon – it will probably end up being cancelled unless it can be reformulated to make it both a lot more attractive and easier.

Project D presents the biggest dilemma of all. Although it appears to be very attractive it is also very difficult to implement. Yet managers will tend to focus on the attractiveness of the project rather than its actual difficulty. And that can occur *even though* they have gone through the force-field and stakeholder analysis thoroughly (see later in this chapter).

When using the AID tool at Hewlett Packard's (HP) mmedical equipment business this happened to one of us twice. Quite separately, two 'D' type projects were identified and as managers spent more time analysing them, commitment to action levels built up.

Although neither of the projects went ahead – in their existing form – both one of us and the (then) internal facilitator, Stuart Reed, had to be relatively strong to convince the teams that some further refinement was necessary.

Stuart Reed said to me at the time:

> *I had gone through with them (the managers) both the implementation forces and the stakeholders. Although it did seem to be an attractive project our two organisational tools were telling us 'it is not going to happen'. I think because the managers were going through the analysis tools for the first time (and hadn't actually tried to implement the project) they hadn't quite realised that it really wasn't going to happen.*

Projects in the north-east zone of the AID grid do present us with some interesting management dilemmas. Following up the HP school of thought, one viewpoint is that it is unlikely to be worthwhile doing these projects as realistically the organisation will lack the commitment to drive them through. However, a second HP school of thought is that such projects merely represent a challenge for creative thinking – as long as they are potentially very attractive it may be very fruitful to do this.

At HP another senior manager re-examined a project with which I had been personally involved some 18 months earlier. This potential project concerned a business process change and a restructuring. At the time the position of this project was due east on the AID grid, that is:

- medium, attractive, and

- very difficult.

This project went into suspended animation for around 18 months. Then, when doing some further work with HP it came to light that the new senior manager had solved the problem both creatively and decisively by out-sourcing the process rather than by internal reorganisation. The project thus shifted from due east to north-west, that is: high attractiveness, low implementation difficulty.

I uncovered a third school of thought working with a Japanese pharma company. Its managing director said to me:

Perhaps we should do that project because *it is difficult.*

A particularly 'cunning plan' is to target projects which, whilst they are likely to be in between very difficult and 'mission impossible' for others to implement, we will find them easier. Here 'mission impossible' is just off the page to the east of the AID grid.

The positionings on the AID grid are likely to be relatively tentative unless tested out using other techniques. For example:

- The 'attractiveness' of the project may require further analysis using value driver and cost driver analysis (see Chapter 5). (Ultimately, this attractiveness can be financially quantified, albeit perhaps approximately.)

- The implementation difficulty can be tested out using force-field analysis and stakeholder analysis (see later in this chapter).

- The difficulty over time can be visualised using the difficulty over time curve (see Chapter 6).

A useful rule of thumb for the less experienced user of the AID grid, or for those who have not used force-field and stakeholder analysis to check out their horizontal positioning, is that:

- if you think the project is easy, it is probably difficult;

- if you think the project is difficult, it is probably very difficult;

- if you think the project is very difficult, it is probably 'mission impossible'.

Another useful technique is to tell scenario stories about the evolution of the project over time in conjunction with the AID grid. This may help to tease out its likely trajectory over time. For example, many projects start out with an assumed north-west position (very attractive and easy), but then zigzag south and east to the south-east (low attractiveness and very difficult).

A final point on AID analysis is that this technique can be used to prioritise each of the bones of the fishbone (or, indeed, the wishbone – see Chapter 3). This can be done either using a separate AID picture or (and this is clever) actually along the edges of the fishbone, as mini-AID pictures with a cross drawn of the positioning.

EXERCISE – AVOIDING 'MISSION IMPOSSIBLE' PROJECTS

Thinking back through your career, ask yourself:

- Which project(s) counts (with hindsight) as 'mission impossible'?
- To what extent could you have anticipated this outcome through scenario story-telling?
- Once the project was under way, what specific danger signs or indicators gave you advance warning that the project might be about to become a 'mission impossible' one?
- What degree of influence did you really have in proactively putting the project onto a different trajectory?

Having dealt thoroughly with AID analysis, let us now turn to force-field analysis, which assesses project implementation difficulty.

Force-field Analysis

Force-field analysis is one of the oldest management tools available and is derived originally from Lewin (1935).

Force-field analysis can be defined as follows:

> *Force-field analysis is the diagnosis and evaluation of enabling and restraining forces that have an impact on the implementation of a project.*

Force-field analysis is a technique which brings to the surface the underlying forces which may pull a particular change forward or which may prevent progress, or even move the change backwards. These 'forces' can be separately identified as 'enablers' or 'constraints'. But neither set of forces can be adequately identified without first specifying the objectives of the pharma project or programme which we focused on in depth in Chapter 3.

When managers first see force-field analysis they often read it as being some form of extended cost-benefit or 'pros and cons' analysis, which it is definitely not. Force-field analysis is simply concerned with the difficulty of the journey which the pharma project is likely to make throughout its implementation.

The difficulty of this journey, like that of any other journey in life, has nothing to do with the attractiveness of reaching the destination. As we have already seen when learning about AID analysis, attractiveness is quite a different concept from difficulty.

The only sense in which it is permissible to incorporate the perceived benefits of the pharma project as a force-field enabler is in so far as:

- there is a actually a genuinely attractive business case for the project *and* one which has turned on key stakeholders; and/or

- that key stakeholders are attracted by the project for other reasons.

Turning back now to force-field analysis, the most effective way of evaluating the forces enabling or constraining achievement of the pharma project objective is to draw this pictorially. This picture represents the relative strength of each individual enabling or constraining force by drawing an arrowed line whose length is in proportion to that relative strength.

A horizontal version of force-field analysis is depicted in Figure 4.6. Note in this case that, on balance, the enabling forces appear less strong than the constraining forces. This particular analysis is for a project to develop a pharma company's strategic plan. It shows that although many of the plans, processes and programmes had been put in place, it was nevertheless difficult to envisage implementation being a complete success. Subsequent events suggest that implementation difficulties at the company were very severe.

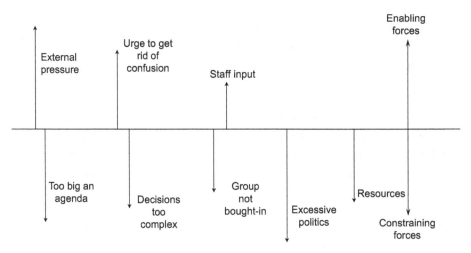

Figure 4.6   Force-field analysis

The example of the pharma company highlights one important truth about force-field analysis, namely that:

> *The degree of ease of the pharma project is only in proportion to the extent of your pre-existing* cunning plan *for implementation.*

Managers who have not already thought hard about the phases of difficulty (see the final exercise in Chapter 3), and about options to get round potential hurdles (for example, push versus pull strategies) may be doomed to suffer a Very Difficult Project.

As a rule of thumb, the enablers should outweigh the constraints by a factor of at least 1.5 to 2 overall, in accordance with the principle of military dominance. Otherwise we should be concerned and potentially worried that implementation 'droop' will set in.

Also, any 'stoppers' (that is, a change that has such a powerful impact that it is likely to stop the project in its tracks) *really must* be addressed, otherwise implementation really won't happen. During (and before) implementation the key implementation forces should be continually monitored to ensure that none threatens to 'go critical' and becomes a 'stopper'.

The next issue that arises is how to evaluate the relative strength of the various forces. Two methods used successfully in the past include:

- scoring each force as having 'high', 'medium' or 'low' impact;

- scoring each force numerically on a scale of 1 to 5.

Where a team may wish to change its mind (and does not wish to spoil its artwork), then by using Post-it® notes, the length of the arrows can be changed.

Most groups of managers work comfortably by using the high, medium or low scoring method. In exceptional cases (for example, where managers have scientific backgrounds or have an inherent love of quantification) the numerical 1 to 5 scale appears to fit more comfortably.

One of the common objections by pharma professionals to force-field analysis is that the whole scoring exercise is 'highly subjective'. This feeling normally occurs within the first ten minutes or so of any analysis exercise. It arises usually because all they have done is to identify that a force is an enabler or a constraint without exploring questions including:

- Why is it an enabler or a constraint?

- How important an influence is it on the change process (and when)?

- What underlying factors does it depend upon in turn?

This highlights that any force-field analysis is dependent on many assumptions, many of which are implicit. A more successful and less 'subjective' analysis will have brought to the surface, shared and agreed these implicit assumptions.

A number of pitfalls need to be avoided in the use of force-field analysis for pharma project management, which include:

- focusing primarily on tangible (as opposed to less tangible) implementation forces;

- missing out major constraints because the team wishes to paint an 'ideal' rather than a realistic picture of the change (we return to these issues in a moment);

- failing to identify a 'stopper'; 'stoppers' should be drawn either as a thick black arrow or, alternatively, as an arrow which goes right to the bottom of the implementation forces analysis and 'off the page'. (This assumes that you are using the vertical format for force-field analysis.)

A 'stopper' can be defined as an influence or change which will effectively put an end to the initiative either through direct confrontation or passive resistance. (Pharma project initiatives may fail because as one constraint is loosened another in effect reasserts itself.) Also, there may be cases where a specific enabling force can be made strong and prove decisive in moving the change forward. This kind of force may be described as an 'unblocker' and can be drawn as a very long (or thick) positive line upwards on the force-field picture.

There may also be instances where a negative and constraining force can be flipped over to make a positive force, and in so doing transform the picture. For instance, if an influential stakeholder (who is currently negative) can be turned around in favour of the change, this can provide a major driver in the pharma project's progress. To prioritise which force to focus on, begin with the most presently limiting (or constraining factor). This is the first key tenet of the *Theory of Constraints* (Goldratt, 1990).

A useful tip is to look beyond the existing enabling forces to the context of the pharma project itself. Within that context, ask yourself whether there are some latent enablers which, if brought to the surface, could be used to unlock organisational energy. For example, if staff feel overburdened with work then a restructuring which is geared not so much to reducing cuts but to *reducing organisational stress and strain* is likely to be most gratefully received.

Or, by using a 'pull' strategy to get staff's ideas on future organisational processes in advance of a restructuring might flush out some really good ideas for simplification. It might also get staff on board as they see these ideas already incorporated in the plans for the new structure.

This is the second, major tenet of the *Theory of Constraints*, which is that within any really difficult situation there is buried somewhere within it some latent, naturally enabling force.

It may be helpful to use the following checklist to brainstorm the enabling or constraining force. This is structured as five categories (based on Peters and Waterman's (1980) original seven 'S's):

- strategy;

- structure;

- style;

- skills;

- systems and resources.

Strategy

- Do we have a simple and clear objective?

- Is this supported by a coherent plan?

- Does this plan fully address the key implementation issues?

Structure

- Are the roles of the key implementors sufficiently clear and well communicated?

- Have they got sufficient power and influence to achieve results?

- Does the project impact on a number of business and/or functional areas and if so, will it be effectively coordinated?

Style

- Does the project require new behaviours in the organisation or changing old behaviours? If so, will these behaviour shifts materialise?

- Is there sufficient commitment to the project, and will this commitment be sustained?

- Does the project team itself have an appropriate leadership and team (with suitable interpersonal and political skills – not just technical)?

Skills

- Does the project require new skills within the organisation and is this being effectively addressed?

- Does the project develop skills which may in turn generate or enable future strategic development opportunities to be detected and exploited?

- Does the project create skills bottlenecks which might either throw other projects off their critical paths, or create internal conflict, or both?

Systems and resources

- Does the project require new systems or processes to achieve success, and will this infrastructure be in place?

- Does the project require significant changes to existing systems or processes and are key stakeholders (the 'guardians' of these systems) on board with *all* of these changes?

- Are there actually *sufficient resources*?

Let us now summarise some of the key 'do's and 'don't's of force-field analysis for pharma projects.

Do

- brainstorm all the key tangible and less tangible forces impacting on the strategic development process;

- include key forces drawn from your from-its analysis (see Chapter 3), and the stakeholder analysis (see later in this chapter);

- test your judgements by questioning 'why?' a force is strong or weak by reference to the strategic implementation objective and by thinking about its constraints within the overall process;

- do the initial force-field analysis on an 'as is' basis – show the problems and be prepared to be provocative;

- where a major constraint exists, draw this in as a stopper (that is as a very long downward arrow) to draw attention to its role in braking the change process;

- use the tool throughout the pharma project management process as the forces will change over time;

- use the force-field for both different sub-projects or activities (as the degree of difficulty will vary) and for separate phases of project implementation;

- involve others to test and provide input to the analysis.

Don't

- confuse force-field analysis with simple cost-benefit analysis – benefits should only be included as a force if they are perceived by and owned by key stakeholders. Often, these benefits are in the eye of the programme initiator and are neutral in driving the change process forward;

- use force-field analysis as a tool just to describe the current position – force-field analysis should be used to re-shape actively your implementation plan to optimise the effect of enabling forces and to neutralise or flip-over the constraining forces to become enablers;

- get bogged down in attempts to evaluate the forces precisely – force-field analysis is a soft science.

Force-field analysis can be used for pharma projects in a number of ways. First, it can be used very formally, either within a team or individually; or, it can be used intuitively – in effect as a form of 'organisational radar'. In fact, having used force-field analysis formally a number of times enables it to become unconscious. However, there are situations when you really do need to revert to a formal picture, if only to get a clearer mirror of your own intuitions.

Stakeholder Analysis

As we saw in the Preface, there will be inevitably more competitive pressure over the next five to ten years due to economic and regulatory conditions, generics and the dilution of the benefits from blockbuster drugs. This will translate itself into much more pressure to deliver projects on time and to cost and within a context of increasing regulation. This will encourage senior managers to compete internally to secure the best resources. It is thus likely, if not inevitable, that getting the right resources will become not only more critical, but more difficult too .In turn, that puts the job of influencing stakeholders at the top of the list of the pharma project manager's priorities.

Stakeholder analysis is another major tool for analysing the implementation difficulty of pharma projects (see Piercey (1989) and Grundy (1993a)).

Having already defined stakeholder analysis at the end of Chapter 3 (and given a preliminary analysis using the stakeholder periscope), we can now focus on its use.

Stakeholder analysis is performed as follows:

1. Identify who you believe the key stakeholders are at any phase of the process (possibly using the stakeholder periscope).

2. Evaluate whether these stakeholders have high, medium or low influence on the issue in question (you need to abstract this from their influence generally in the organisation).

3. Evaluate whether at the current time they are for the project, against it, or idling in 'neutral'.

Stakeholder analysis is particularly important for pharma projects because of both internal organisational complexity, with projects often being managed across borders, and also due to the need to understand external stakeholders, like the national health service, regulations and patients.

In order to estimate where a stakeholder is positioned approximately, you will need to see the world from that particular stakeholder's perspective. From experience over the years we have found that the best way to convey this is to ask managers to have in effect an 'out-of-body-experience' – but not quite literally, of course!

This involves not merely trying to sense the surface attitudes of stakeholders to a particular issue but also the deeper-seated emotions, focus, anxieties and even prejudices.

We will reserve a more detailed treatment of how to do this later in Chapter 7 on 'Influencing People and Behaviour'. In this chapter we will illustrate how a specific stakeholder's agenda can be mapped using stakeholder agenda analysis, which is another application of force-field analysis.

To bring home the point that stakeholder analysis *really does* involve having the out-of-body experience, I usually go as far as even showing a picture of the two television stars of the *X-Files*, Mulder and Scully! – From experience, managers who *literally do* take the perspective that 'I *am* the stakeholder' are typically at least 50 per cent more accurate in their analysis.

The above-mentioned three steps give a good 'first cut' of the pattern of stakeholders. The cluster of stakeholders depicted on a stakeholder grid (see Figure 4.7) should then be assessed to see what the overall picture looks like, particularly:

• Is the project an easy bet?

• Or is it highlighting a long slog?

• Or, finally, does this seem like 'mission impossible'?

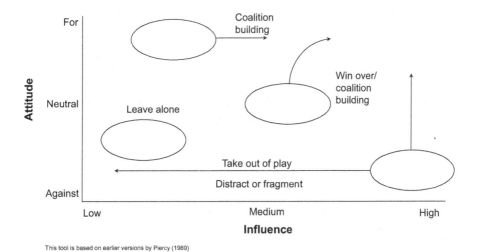

This tool is based on earlier versions by Piercy (1989)

Figure 4.7   Stakeholder analysis

For instance, if most of the stakeholders are clustered towards the bottom part of the stakeholder grid, then you clearly have a 'mission impossible' on your hands (unless the stakeholders can be repositioned).

Another difficult configuration is where there is an equal number of supporting stakeholders (with lower influence), that is, in the north-west of the picture, to those against (but having higher influence) – in the south-east. Once again, this means that the pharma project is likely to experience major implementation difficulties.

Finally, where you have a large number of stakeholders floating in neutral in the middle of the picture, this very neutrality can present major problems due to organisational inertia.

It is a particularly useful idea to position yourself on the stakeholder grid, especially if you are the project manager. This helps you to re-examine your own position – and your underlying agendas – which may be mixed.

Following your tentative, first-cut analysis you should then move on to the next phase of your pharma project:

1.   Can new stakeholders be brought into play to shift the balance of influence or can existing players be withdrawn in some way (or be subtly distracted)?

2.   Is it possible to boost the influence of stakeholders who are currently in favour of the project?

3.   Is it possible to reduce the influence of any antagonistic stakeholders?

4.   Can coalitions of stakeholders in favour be achieved so as to strengthen their combined influence?

5.   Can coalitions of stakeholders antagonistic to the project be prevented?

6.   Can the project change itself, in appearance or in substance, be reformulated to diffuse hostility to it?

7.   Are there possibilities of 'bringing on board' any negative stakeholders by allowing them a role or in incorporating one or more of their prized ideas?

8.   Is the pattern of influence of stakeholders sufficiently hostile for the project to warrant its re-definition?

An example of stakeholder analysis in use is contained in Figure 4.8. This is again based on the position as assessed by internal managers of players at the same pharma company for which we drew up a force-field analysis earlier.

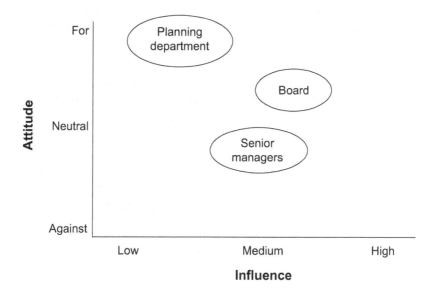

Figure 4.8   Stakeholder analysis – an example

Once you have done the stakeholder analysis it may well be worthwhile re-visiting the force-field analysis to either introduce one, or more, new forces, or to revise earlier views. The force-field analysis will now incorporate *all* of the enabling and constraining forces, including some of the more political and the less tangible ones.

Often a particular stakeholder may be difficult to position. This may be because his/her agendas might be complex. It is quite common to find that it is only one specific blocker which has made a stakeholder into an influential antagonist.

Where there are very large numbers of stakeholders at play on a particular pharma issue, this may invite some simplification of the project. For instance, the project may need to be refined, perhaps even stopped and then restarted, in order to resolve an organisational mess.

In order to use stakeholder analysis effectively you may need to set some process arrangements in place where a team project is involved. First, the analysis may be usefully performed in a 'workshop' environment so as to give the analysis a 'reflective' or 'learning' feel. This will help to integrate managers' thinking on a key project. It may also be useful to devise code-words for key stakeholders in order to make the outputs from this change tool feel 'safe'. On several occasions managers have decided to adopt nicknames for the key players. An element of humour will help to diffuse the potential seriousness of performing stakeholder analysis.

So far we have used stakeholder analysis in a relatively static manner. But obviously key stakeholders are likely to shift over time – and early support for the project may therefore evaporate. A number of things need to be anticipated therefore, namely:

- Senior managers' support is likely to be very sensitive to the perceived ongoing success of the pharma project as it evolves. Any signs of failure are likely to be accompanied by suddenly diminishing support.

- New stakeholders may enter the scene, and others might disappear.

- Certain stakeholders may increase in influence, or even decrease in influence.

- Where the project changes in its scope or in its focus significantly, stakeholders will then change their positions.

- Stakeholders' own agendas might change due to external factors outside this particular project. For example other projects might distract them or result in a reprioritisation of agendas and of this project in particular.

Due to the above it may be necessary to review stakeholder positions *several times at least* during the lifetime of the project.

As a final note, obviously the stakeholder tool should not be used for covert personal and political purposes. Its purpose is to help get things done in organisations and not to obtain personal advantage for its own sake.

For further analysis it is possible to examine how stakeholders may change over time by plotting:

- their attitude over time (ranging from 'against' through to 'for'); and

- their influence over time (ranging from 'for' through to 'against').

This is depicted in Figure 4.9.

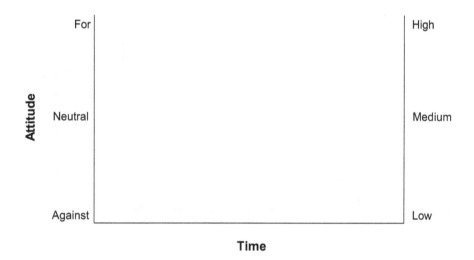

Figure 4.9   Stakeholder attitude and influence over time curves

For instance, in drug development a whole raft of different stakeholders will be involved in phases I, II, III and IV, and also within each key aspect of the project within each phase.

Further, it is possible to prioritise which stakeholders to focus on by plotting:

- *their* level of influence on this issue; and

- *our* degree of influence over them.

In Figure 4.9 we see the two axes plotted. Note that one should try to evolve strategies for gaining more influence over those stakeholders who are more influential – and who we have currently *least* influence over.

In Figure 4.10 we now see a force-field analysis picture used to represent the turn-ons and turn-offs within a single stakeholder's agenda (for a job move to another pharma company). This is not useful to do for others, but also for yourself.

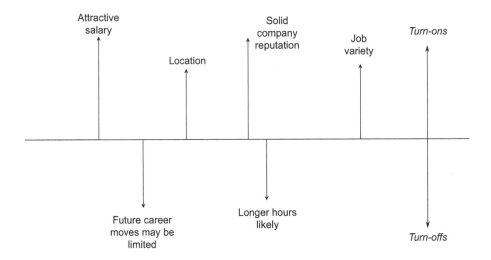

Figure 4.10   Stakeholder agenda analysis of a new job

As a final note, do not think of each stakeholder in isolation. Frequently one stakeholder's positioning is interdependent with the position of others. This can be drawn out by clustering independent stakeholders on a flipchart and then drawing lines between those who are most interdependent with one another.

'How–how' and Work Breakdown Structure Analysis

So far we have been working at the project level. Whilst we may have thought in broad terms about a project's overall implementation, this may well not have been broken down into detailed actions. This task can be achieved by 'how–how' analysis. (This is also known as 'work breakdown structure' (WBS) –

a term we do not prefer to use as it sounds rather mechanistic. This might also fail to imply that one needs to be highly imaginative in detecting *all* the tasks needed to achieve the result, as opposed to the just more obvious activities.)

How–how analysis works by starting off with the core task, such as to turn around a business (see Figure 4.11). This begins at the left-hand side of the page. By working from left to right, we repeatedly ask the question: 'How is that particular task to be achieved?'.

This produces more and more detail until a complete listing of activities is created. Whilst at this stage these activities are not phased over time, this should give a really detailed idea of project activities.

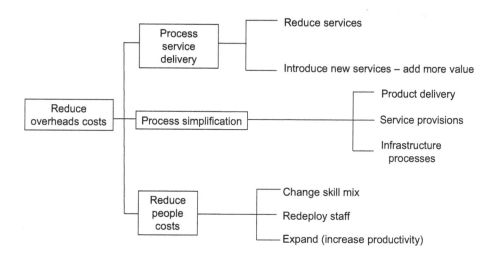

Figure 4.11   'How–how' analysis

With how–how analysis it is crucial to expand the activities to those softer areas which may also be required to achieve the required result. This might entail training or other support for behavioural or mind-set change.

In the pharma industry 'how–how' analyses (or work breakdown analyses) frequently omit the softer factors which will need to be addressed to make the project effective. These include, for example, positioning, communication, training and team-building.

Once the major activities have been generated the next stage is to begin to think about phasing them over time. This can be done in either of two ways:

- where there are relatively few interdependencies in the sequencing of activities you can go directly to a Gantt chart, which displays activities over particular times; or,

- where there are likely to be extensive interdependencies in the sequencing of activities you might seek instead to develop the 'activity network'.

A Gantt chart (named after its creator) is shown in Figure 4.12 for the business turnaround specific pharma project. Note that many of the activities occur in parallel with one another.

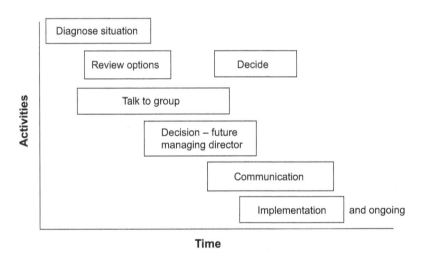

Figure 4.12   Gantt chart: Pharmaceutical business turnaround

Gantt analysis is normally very easy to use. Even where there might be a complex underlying network of opportunities it may still be worthwhile doing a quick Gantt chart to get a 'feel' for when things may need to happen.

Once again, we should not see Gantt analysis as a mechanistic process, for there are frequently many possible phasings of these activities. Even where there are well-trodden ways of doing particular kinds of projects, such as clinical research projects in the pharma industry, there are still often choices as to when activities can begin, and in what order.

This also raises the interesting issue of project management as a way of increasing time-based competitive advantage (Stalk, 1990). In most industries it is becoming increasingly important to accelerate the implementation of business strategies. Given the greater competitive pressure on the pharma industry – which we saw earlier – there are some very real challenges to the time it takes typically to complete projects and phases. These typically warrant some re-engineering of the generic processes (especially in drug development/ clinical trials) which projects are expected to move through.

Projects, as we have already defined them, are all about achieving a pre-targeted result in a specific time and at a specific cost. It is therefore imperative to see what we can do (through Gantt chart analysis, and through the activity network and the critical path) to accelerate these.

A very solid rule of thumb which might help us to achieve this is:

Try to do activities sooner than you might otherwise think of doing.

This rule of thumb applies especially to activities which are more likely to be on the critical path, and those which are most constraining.

Accelerating projects in the pharma industry seems therefore to behave as follows. Up to a certain point there are some very real cost savings (due to time and resource saved) as you accelerate activities. But after that point, the costs go up, sometimes quite disproportionately – as errors are made and costs are generated elsewhere or later, or because resources get in the way of each other. Another rule is: if you accelerate, then you really must simplify!

Another possibility in activity analysis is delay. Whilst this may not be an obvious strategy sometimes it may be wise to delay an activity if there are simply too many activities happening at once. When you try to do a number of things simultaneously efficiency quickly declines after a certain point.

If, therefore, particular activities do not need to be done at the present time, a temporary delay may actually help to accelerate other activities disproportionately. In the pharma industry the prevailing mindset in senior management often is one of 'we need to do all of these projects, now, and all at once,' rather than acknowledging that this will fragment efforts, and be counterproductive in the long-run.

Indeed, there is invariably a good deal more flexibility within the activity analysis of *when* things need to get done by. The major constraining factors are not so much performing the activities but the availability of data, decisions being made, resources being made actually available, and sheer physical constraints. For these factors are most constraining for the pharma project, rather than necessarily the activities themselves.

Critical Path (and Uncertainty) Analysis

The 'critical path' is that sequence of activities which currently takes the longest, and which, if delayed, is likely to delay the entire project.

Critical path analysis is at the very centre of traditional project management. Whilst being absolutely imperative for complex, pharma projects – which are typically complex at a technical level – it needs to be set in context amongst the other tools in its degree of importance when considering any project. Whilst there is, invariably, a real critical path for a project, this is frequently likely to crystallise during the project rather than before it.

If you have already done an approximate Gantt chart this will give you some strong clues to the likely structure of the network of activities of the project. Essentially, you will need to decide which activity needs to be done, in what order. So, for each activity you need to work out which activities had to have been completed already *in order for* this activity to be started. You can build up a chain or network of activities quite quickly. One useful way of doing this is to write each activity on a Post-it® note and then simply place in the appropriate order on a flipchart. Then, once you have the order sorted out, draw in the arrows to represent the activity path through the activity network.

Alternatively, the Post-it® notes can be arranged on an urgency-importance grid (see Figure 4.13), which is another classic, albeit 'quick and dirty' way for prioritising pharma project activities. With this grid it is important to avoid over-focusing on the most urgent at the expense of the most important. The grid can also help you in time management. For example, spend 80 per cent of your time on the few, really important projects, focusing on them all at once. Then spend the remaining 20 per cent of your time (on dedicated days or half-days) specialising in clearing the less important projects before they become too urgent and distracting.

Using Post-it® notes is a good way of testing one's assumptions about the relative order in which the key activities need to be carried out. Using this process one is often able to parallel work activities which might previously have been assumed were strictly sequential, for instance. Figure 4.12 now gives us a network of activities for a business turnaround plan.

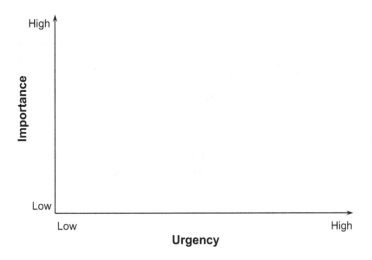

Figure 4.13   Urgency–importance grid

Turning now to the critical path of the project, we need to identify that sequence of activities which, if subject to any delay at all, will delay the whole project itself. This is actually what the critical path really is. So, for example, in Figure 4.14 we now see the duration of activities and that path C is therefore the critical path.

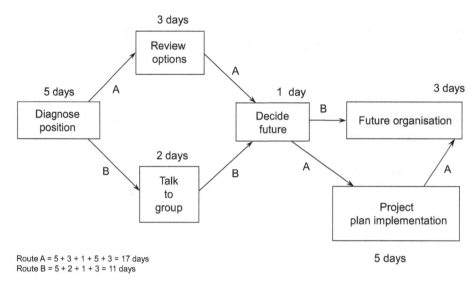

Route A = 5 + 3 + 1 + 5 + 3 = 17 days
Route B = 5 + 2 + 1 + 3 = 11 days

Figure 4.14   Project network: A business turnaround

With pharma projects it is often less obvious not only which sequence of activities is the critical path, but also how determinate this path will be. In real life the critical path will shift considerably for a pharma project, operating in an incremental and often turbulent organisational environment so characteristic of the pharma industry today.

Whilst it is useful to have some view as to what the most likely critical path is for a pharma project, it is equally important to:

- monitor the key uncertainties;

- identify the most constraining factors of data, decisions, resource and physical constraints;

- be aware of whether any activities can be accelerated internally – to make up for the delay;

- be aware of whether deploying additional resources (possibly out-sourced) can be brought in, in order to accelerate key activities;

- be aware of which activities frequently take longer than assumed – especially softer activities like shifting mind-set and behaviours.

Some specific examples of questions which can be used to help shorten the critical path for a clinical reward project are as follows:

- Which phase II studies must be completed before starting the first phase III study?

- Can phase III be started based on an analysis of phase II studies, rather than waiting for their final clinical report?

- Which are the fastest countries for starting and completing clinical trials?

- How can you ensure timely sign-off of key documents such as protocols, contracts and so on?

- Could you use a site management organisation (SMO) to enable you to recruit study sites faster?

- What stability-supported shelf life of the formulation is needed before the start of a particular study?

- How can the study evaluation be expedited, for example, by using a CRO or using remote data entry?

- Is it possible to increase the assumed patient enrolment rate to reduce the time to finish a study?

- Which task is likely to overrun the estimated duration because of unexpected technical problems and can this risk be reduced by adding resources early?

This makes critical path analysis a much more flexible process for pharma projects. Indeed, it becomes just as much a 'soft', intuitive process as much as an analytical process.

In order to assess the relative *difficulty* of specific activities, it may well be useful to draw up mini-force-field analysis to get a better feel for this. This will help to identify those activities which may require either more time, more resources or simply more thinking through (bringing us back once more to the 'cunning plan').

Moving now on to uncertainty, our classic technique for managing and monitoring this is Mitroff's 'uncertainty–importance grid' (see Figure 4.15). This grid can be used for a variety of pharma projects, including:

- new drug development;

- clinical trials;

- new market entry and new products;

- acquisitions and alliances;

- operational improvements (for example, IT/business processes);

- organisational restructuring and change.

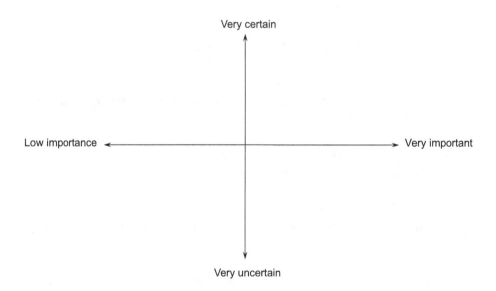

Figure 4.15   Uncertainty–importance grid

We will return to the grid in Chapter 5 'Evaluating Pharmaceutical Projects'.

The grid case is used specifically for surfacing the assumptions underlying the particular activity. The grid plots the degree of importance horizontally against degree of uncertainty vertically. Once again, use Post-it® notes to represent the key assumptions and then position them on the grid.

Probably the majority of your chosen assumptions will end up between the centre and the right of the grid – that is from medium to high importance. This is not a problem as long as you do capture some of the assumptions which are of lower importance, for quite frequently these lower importance assumptions increase in importance either as you think harder about their implications for the activity or just as they shift during the project.

Not only might the assumptions shift from left to right but they are also likely to move from top to bottom as uncertainty increases. The most dangerous assumptions are obviously in the south-east: both most important *and* most uncertain.

In defining your assumptions the usual convention is to think of the world as 'going right'. In other words, these are the assumptions which need to be fulfilled in order for project success to be successful. From experience, many pharma managers seem to find working with assumptions like this surprisingly difficult. To some extent I believe this is due to the in-built optimism that managers have: a culture of 'before it goes wrong, our only assumption is that it will go right'. This seems also coupled with the phenomenon once described as 'the Nietzsche Syndrome' or 'the Will to Power'. That is, if it goes wrong we will just get on and fix it. (Nietzsche was a famous German philosopher who focused on mental strength as a source of power.)

Risk is a future event which results in negative consequence (to cost, schedule, product profile, or other constraint). Risk Management is the systematic application of policies, procedures, methods and practices to the tasks of *identifying, analysing, evaluating, handling* and *monitoring* risk.

Risk Management aims to *avoid and minimise uncertainty*, thereby increasing the likelihood of achieving the project's objectives. It is a proactive process and should be employed on all projects undertaken. If you manage the risk you manage the project.

To identify risk the following approaches are used:

- look at CPA (Critical Path Activities);

- ask people in the team;

- work by Murphy's Law – 'anything that can go wrong will go wrong' – test out assumptions and consider the project environment, future scenarios;

- risk profile:

  - industry specific requirements, for example, clinical research – IMP delivery, EC and regulatory approval
  - organisational requirements – for example, internal sign offs

- historical records

  - planned versus actual performance
  - problem/risk log
  - post project review

Examples of risks in the pharma industry include:

- regulatory:

  - approvals
  - filings
  - inadequate regulatory intelligence

- CMC:

  - formulation
  - process
  - analytics
  - stability
  - scale-up
  - transfer
  - packaging
  - reimportation
  - other

- preclinical:

  - existing data
  - proposed work
  - other

- clinical/medical:

  - clinical development plan
  - target population
  - safety
  - ethical approval
  - reimportation
  - other

- marketing:

  - costs
  - competition
  - market assessment
  - forecasting
  - pricing
  - launch
  - reimportation
  - other

- sales:

  - costs
  - customer assessment
  - forecasting
  - pricing
  - launch
  - reimportation
  - other

- management/organisation:

  - team
  - systems/technologies
  - intellectual property
  - organisation
  - planning
  - project management
  - senior management
  - culture

The ways of managing risk are as follows:

- Avoid: eliminate the root cause.

- Mitigate: reduce the value of a risk by reducing its *impact* or its *probability* of occurrence.

- Accept: assume the risk without engaging in special activities to manage it *(all accepted moderate and high risks must have a contingency plan)*.

- Transfer: assign the risk to another entity to achieve an overall reduction in project risk, for example, transfer to CRO in the pharma industry.

Managing risk can be dealt with as follows:

- determine probability that the risk event will occur;

- determine impact to the project goal if the risk event occurs;

- prioritise risks using risk (probability x impact) matrix;

- assign each risk response activity a risk owner;

- consider organisation attitude toward risk.

Monitoring the risk is very important and should include:

- continually tracking and evaluating the performance of risk response actions against established metrics;

- taking corrective action where necessary to bring the project back in line with the plan;

- responding to risk event triggers by implementing contingency plans if needed;

For each risk the following steps should be in place:

- an assessment of the nature of the risk and the exposure to the risk based upon the impact and probability of the risk occurring;

- Actions that are planned to control and manage the risks. This is described in terms of the responses developed for the risks identified, the actions already taken and the degree of completion of the responses to the risks required (operational, strategic and financial) and the timelines involved.

- Who is responsible for managing each of the risks.

- How each risk will be monitored.

- An awareness of risk triggers. A risk trigger is a sign or symptom which signals that a risk is likely to materialise. For example, initial poor recruitment would be a risk trigger for risk attached to completing the trial behind schedule.

- Good communication throughout!

Another way of managing uncertainty and risk is to use the risk register (see Figure 4.16). This takes a slightly different approach to the uncertainty–importance grid (Figure 4.15). The risk register:

- assesses probability;

- also identifies remedial management action.

The risk register is thus particularly useful where probabilities can be assessed – and with reasonable accuracy. It is also a good way of documenting risk, and also of getting pharma managers to think ahead and to try to head-off future project difficulties.

Returning now to activity analysis, activities which have a heavy concentration of assumptions in the danger zone (or south-east of the uncertainty–importance grid) are very likely to suffer:

Work breakdown structure ref./activity	Risk	Probability	Effect/ impact	Management action
1				
2				
3				
4				

Figure 4.16   Risk register

- delays;

- uneven delivery of results;

- additional costs;

- knock-on difficulties on to other activities, or even onto other projects.

The uncertainty–importance grid thus helps to identify the really 'hot-spot' activities throughout the project, enabling us to helicopter over it. It also identifies, in the south-east zone of the grid, where we should collect any data deciding on whether to do the pharma project or not.

The uncertainty–importance grid can thus be used to check the robustness of the critical path analysis. For example, what happens to the critical path if hot-spot activities exceed their projected durations by 20 per cent or 30 per cent? This enables almost certain blockages to be foreseen, along with their knock-on effects.

Clearly, only a foolish project manager would operate with no slack to accommodate for activity over-runs. It is essential, one way or another, to build in some oxygen or 'float' to the project. 'Float' is defined as the amount of time allowed for over-run of activities.

This 'float' can be built-in either as a final activity to the project (that is, explicitly), or by particular generous time allowances for one or more activities. Another approach is to deliberately front-load the time pressure on early stage activities so that should slippage occur then you are still actually on schedule. Minor apparent slippage actually has the effect of stimulating concentration and effort which, if it is not present at the early stages of a project, is hardly likely to be there at the later stages.

If one allows deliberately more time for a project activity then there is an opposite result. Not only this, but it is almost incredible how wasteful managers can be if given luxurious time targets.

For example, one workshop facilitator in a pharma company mistakenly gave a team not 45 minutes to achieve a task but an hour and 15 minutes. After about 15 minutes (a third through the activity), hardly anything had been accomplished. In fact the managers kept drinking coffee for five minutes. After 30 minutes the teams had just got started and were rambling around the issues.

When the facilitator prompted them about progress, they simply turned around and said, 'Well, we have 45 minutes to go.' The moral of this is: if you give people a lot of time then they will take it!

Returning now to critical path analysis, project software (like Microsoft Project) is of some value in helping work through the potential implications of project delay. But a serious word of warning is needed here. Managers who are inexperienced in project management or those who are not so familiar with the special challenges of managing pharma projects, may become too engrossed in playing with activity spreadsheets. It is all too easy to make project management into rocket science, which it rarely needs to be.

Another project methodology which has gained significant currency in the pharma industry is PRINCE. According to one pharma manager:

> *What PRINCE has done is to establish some standards for managing the planning stage of projects. But the requirements of PRINCE require supplementing by more visual/qualitative thinking too.*

Critical path and activity analysis leads us on naturally to the topic of resource management. You can produce a fabulous-looking project plan – but also one that is hopelessly unrealistic considering resource constraints.

Imagine, for example, a situation where a number of activities have been scheduled in parallel within a certain time period. Figure 4.16 shows this in relation to the availability of resources. At the mid-part of the activity there is a big resource gap which, if not filled, could lead to a significant delay in the project. Indeed, the ceiling of available resource may not necessarily be flat, but itself undulating and changing over time, depending upon:

- holidays, sickness and training;

- new joiners or leavers;

- staff working on other projects elsewhere;

- the ability to source-in extra skills from outside – either as consultants or as sub-contractors.

Again, project software (with suitably injected intelligent assumptions) should flag any resource gaps – at least in terms of quantity (if not the quality) of skills missing.

We have found (when facilitating pharma project planning) that quite often these dips in resource availability are not typically well factored into the process.

We should now add a final note on activity and critical path analysis. Highly elaborate project plans (especially those compiled using computer software) can give the impression that everything will just happen on time. But one of the most critical assumptions is the actual release of resources to the project on a just-in-time basis. Where these resources come from a general pool of resources or from another specific department then one cannot simply assume that staff *will* be available to start on time. Even where they work on projects within the same department, they may be delayed in completing other projects.

So, you need to establish check-points in the pharma project plan to double-check that future resources will be available, and when assumed. This will not only highlight potential bottlenecks in advance but may also help accelerate activities in other projects so that staff can be made available – as has been assumed.

Often the process of resource allocation will not go very smoothly. There will be real conflicts which may not be resolved by just mere 'horse-trading'. This problem underscores the importance of prioritising projects effectively, and also the assessment of the costs of delay.

'Costs of delay' is a fundamental concept for pharma project management. Costs of delay can be defined as:

The total costs, both directly and indirectly (and tangible and less tangible) of delay in a project relative to each unit of time.

Costs of delay are well understood in at least some industries, such as in oil exploration (where delay exacts penalty charges) and in major construction projects. They are often extremely critical in the pharma industry where delay for a drug launch can cost a considerable amount of money per day. Notwithstanding this, our perception is that many pharma projects are subjected to quite arbitrary resource (and cost) constraints, which far exceed the costs of delivery.

In particular, an assessment of these costs does not seem to be used extensively during earlier stages of the drug's developmental cycle. Some projects are therefore starved of resource – with considerable costs of delay, especially during clinical trials of new drugs.

Finally, it is crucial during the project planning phase to perform an overview of the key interdependencies which each pharma project has on others within the organisation. This can be achieved by again writing down on Post-it® notes the names of key projects and then clustering them on a flipchart. The strong interdependencies between projects can be drawn in as thick, bold arrows, whilst the weaker interdependencies are drawn in as dotted arrows. An example of a project interdependency map is illustrated in Figure 4.17. In view of the complexities of project activities and of project interdependencies we will look next at project management software.

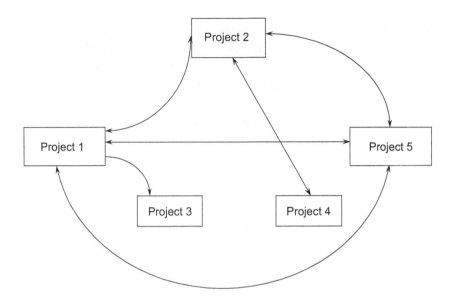

Figure 4.17   Project interdependency map

Project Management Software

The 'so what' from the above sections is that drug development projects are quite diverse and therefore require individual and highly specific project strategies.

There are a number of commercial packages available that track the progress of a clinical trial from the clinical plan through to the medical report and publication. Such systems are able to hold information on all aspects of the trial covering clinical plans, protocols, sponsor and CRO (if applicable) personnel involved, investigators, monitoring activities including checklists and reports.

These packages have the potential to assist in reducing delays and highlighting overdue actions. Databases are able to hold details of all the current, planned and completed studies, then this information can be used to help in planning future studies. Additional information such as clinical trial supplies, finance and documentation modules can be added to the database

By covering all trial phases and being a shared system, they can significantly improve communication between members of the international clinical programme. Clinical managers can study the progress of studies and analyse anticipated resource requirements.

One of the best-known clinical trials software packages available is the International Management Package for the Administration of Clinical Trials (IMPACT). This system can calculate estimated manpower requirements for each country from basic information about the trial. The clinical trial supplies function includes the ability to track and manage medication supplies, checking batch numbers, labelling and expiry dates. Trials can be entered on to the system years before they are due to start and if changes are made in the development programme the system can easily be amended to take account of these. The package runs on an industry standard range of hardware (mainframes, client-server monitors) and uses, in common with many other systems, ORACLE as the core database.

In addition to IMPACT there are an increasing number of software systems now available to support clinical development activities. Such systems are frequently able to provide planning and management of drug development including studies from phase I to IV at head office and affiliates. Systems are available which allow checklists of activities as specified in individual companies SOPs to be put on the system. Several of these systems use ORACLE as the core database (which is widely used by the pharma industry) and interface to a wide range of third-party packages for decision support graphics, projects planning, spreadsheets and desktop publishing.

Some of the systems available which support the clinical development programme have the following facilities:

- To assist with all tasks involved in monitoring investigator sites by Clinical Research Associates (CRA) monitors. Such systems use user-friendly Microsoft Windows-based software that runs on notebook computers. These systems help monitors and CRAs with preparing visit reports, patient tracking, CRF tracking, supplies reconciliation, logging adverse events and tracking investigator payments.

- Data management systems can help simplify CRF design, data entry screen design, database set-up, and checking the quality of data entered.

- Adverse event reporting within the sponsor drug safety unit is also available in some of these systems. Adverse events can be logged directly to a safety database. Adverse events can be tracked and coded according to standard dictionaries such as MedDRA (Medical Dictionary for Regulatory Activities). Adverse events can be assessed for severity, causality and outcome. Standard reports are then generated to be sent to regulatory authorities using the required standard formats (for example, Council for International Organization of Medical Sciences (CIOMS) or yellow card).

Many of the commercial pharma specific systems are sophisticated but expensive and are mainly used by the larger pharma companies. However, there are many less expensive computer-based project analysis tools available, such as Microsoft Project, which are frequently used by pharma companies and CROs.

Project management software is constantly changing with new products and new versions of old products are regularly available. Some of the products which is used in the pharma industry include the following:

Table 4.1   Project management software

Product	Supplier
Artemis	Lucas Management Systems
Autoplan	Digital Tools Inc
ClinSite	ClinLogic
Cobra	Welcome Software
Interactive Trial Management Solutions	ICTI
IMPACT	FW Pharma Systems
MacProject	Apple Computer
MasterTrial	Clinical Control Ltd
Microsoft Project	Microsoft
Milestones	Kidasa Software
Project Planner	Primavera
SMART	Datapharm Australia
Time Line	Timeline Solutions

Conclusion

Developing project strategy and plans can be a relatively complex process, even once the project's overall scope has been defined. This phase of pharma project management necessitates drawing together traditional techniques of project management (such as activity and critical path analysis) with the more strategic techniques of AID analysis, force-field analysis, stakeholder analysis and the uncertainty–importance grid.

We have now seen how pharma project management is very far from being analytically straightforward, even when deploying the additional techniques which we have run through.

To perform a more detailed project evaluation, however, we will need additional techniques from scenario development and from finance and shareholder value theory.

5

Evaluating Pharmaceutical Projects

Introduction

Pharma projects are inevitably subject to the compounding effects of uncertainty over time. This makes it more difficult to perform an effective appraisal of them, especially in financial terms. Paradoxically, the traditional approach of finance theory has been to pretend almost that such uncertainty does not exist. By focusing almost exclusively on the need to quantify value (and with precision) financial theory has turned the financial appraisal of pharma projects virtually into a ritual.

In the past, perhaps, strategic management has (with certain exceptions) gone into a retreat and allowed a financial perspective to become perhaps too dominant. In this chapter we seek much closer integration of strategic and financial appraisal for pharma projects.

Most major pharma projects require – sooner or later – a considerable amount of investment, whether this is capitalised on the company's balance sheet or not. Often managers see doing the business case as a chore, especially when they have already gone past the point of 'no-return' in their minds as to whether to do it or not. Where there is a lag between making the strategic commitment and the preparation of a business case, this may put a further psychological distance between the strategic thinking and the financial analysis. This implies therefore that both strategic and financial appraisal of projects needs to be fully integrated within a single decision-making process.

In evaluating any pharma project we must therefore take a closer look at the decision-making process which might apply to a more complex pharma project, as follows (see Figure 5.1):

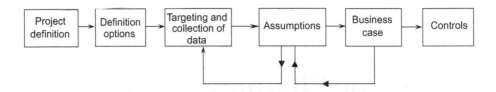

Figure 5.1   Pharmaceutical project evaluation

- Project definition: Define the scope and focus of the pharma project, including its strategic objectives and context (as already seen in Chapter 3).

- Definition options: Explore critical options for the decision and also any options which it forecloses (see Chapter 4).

- Targeting and collection of data: Target data required having done a first-cut review of the kind of external and internal assumptions which will need to be made about key value drivers.

- Assumptions evaluation: Collect and evaluate data through formulating the external and internal assumptions. Test these assumptions and re-visit the key options and work-up contingency plans.

- Business case: Present the business case and, where feasible, refine the programme to add more value at less cost and at lowest risk.

- Controls: Translate the business case into monitoring measures and controls.

Understanding the Business Value System

But before we examine this process stage-by-stage, we need to examine in more depth how value is created in business as part of a system which we can call the 'business value system'.

The business value system can be defined as:

The set of interdependent situations within a business which either directly or indirectly adds value to the customer and ultimately generates a net cash inflow.

The business value system provides a context against which the value of pharma projects can be assessed.

The business value system is also more informative than simply talking about a 'business model', as it (a) focuses explicitly on value; (b) focuse on value creation as a system, and (c) specifically sets out to exploit interdependencies.

An example of a business value system is illustrated in Figure 5.2. This shows the impact of an IT project aimed at improving data capture. The key value creating activities represented in Figure 5.2 show:

- increased accuracy of data recording;

- ease of demonstrating regulatory compliance;

- possible, reduction in costs *ongoing* of administration;

- improved decision-taking (for example in achieving the milestones set by clinical projects in time);

- provision of cost data for monitoring project costs.

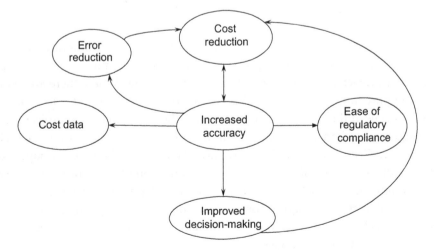

Figure 5.2   Business value system: IT project for data capture

Note here that increased accuracy of data recording feeds into the regulatory compliance process. Also, increased accuracy of data recording leads to some further reduction in costs via eliminating errors. Improved decision-making also further reduces costs. Whilst this is a relatively simple business value system it nevertheless helps to show how a pictorial method of visualising the project's context, and its interdependent value flows, is a healthy antecedent before 'doing the numbers'.

By mapping out the business value system and showing where a project concept impacts both now and in the future, we can more easily understand how the project adds value.

We will return to the business value system during our later discussions of assumptions surrounding the declining base case.

Stages in Pharmaceutical Project Appraisal

In this section we go through each one of the stages in the earlier pharma project appraisal process (definition, options, targeting and collection of data, assumptions evaluation).

PROJECT DEFINITION

We have already explored project definition extensively within Chapter 3, 'Defining Pharmaceutical Projects', but now we need to turn to the linkages between this definition and financial appraisal.

First, if we examine the definition of the decision (or programme) more clearly we soon realise there are many problems in defining the unit of analysis. Is it a particular project or a more broadly-based programme? Where there are many and complex interdependencies it is frequently easier and better to evaluate the financials at the level of a set of projects ('the pharmaceutical project set' – see Figure 5.3). (Remember that we examined key project interdependencies in the section 'Critical Path (and Uncertainty) Analysis' at the end of Chapter 4.) This requires analysis of the project in relation to other areas of the business. For example there may be a new drug being developed in a pharma company for the equivalent of a Viagra – for women. This might complement an existing drug for tackling male impotency problems – particularly in terms of its marketing and brand synergies.

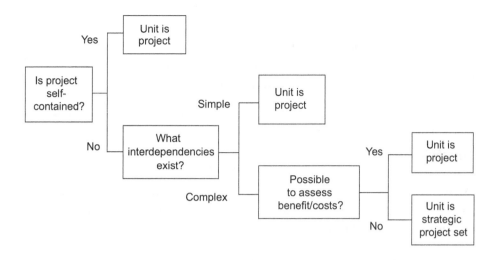

Figure 5.3   Defining the pharmaceutical project set

One of the biggest traps in evaluating project decisions is, therefore, to analyse projects at an inappropriate level. Figure 5.3 suggests that you first need to question whether the project is self-contained or not. Only if it is self-contained can you – at that point – determine that it should be analysed as a distinct project.

Next, you need to ask whether there are many interdependencies, and, if so, are these simple (thus enabling them to be analysed as a discrete project) or are they complex? If they are complex then the final question is 'is it easy to do a cost/benefit analysis of them?' If it is not easy, then you should *not* analyse this as a separate project. Instead, you should analyse it amongst part of a higher level set of projects, or the 'programme' which we described earlier.

EXERCISE – DEFINING THE LEVEL OF EVALUATION FOR A MAJOR PHARMACEUTICAL PROJECT

For one major pharma project you are involved in (or have been involved with in the past year), ask yourself:

- Is the project relatively self-contained (or not)?
- Are their many interdependencies which impact on its value?

- Are these interdependencies simple or complex?
- Are these interdependencies feasible to quantify?
- Should we appraise the project at the level of the project set, or as integral part of the business strategy?

DEFINITION OPTIONS

As we saw in the early part of Chapter 4, there are invariably many different options for defining any pharma project – all of which have major financial implications. For instance:

- Should the strategic objective be achieved through organic or through acquisitive activity?

- Is it more appropriate to move forward on the project very quickly or slowly?

- Is it worthwhile piloting its development prior to making a bigger commitment?

- Should commitment be delayed until there is a sufficiently strong implementation capability, enough resource, and perhaps better timing?

- Can the project's key objectives be fulfilled at lower cost, or with greater flexibility through an alternative option?

And, finally:

- If we go ahead with this particular project, what other options (present and future) does this decision foreclose?

Going back to the beginning of Chapter 4, the project option grid is a useful way of scoping options and their potential attractiveness prior to getting involved in more detailed analysis.

TARGETING AND COLLECTION OF DATA

Once you have identified one or more options you should then identify the data required in order to assess the cash flow impact of any investment in the project.

Data can be collected from a variety of sources, particularly:

Externally

- From external distribution channels (for example, health authorities, hospitals, pharmacists, and so on) or patients by understanding whether any project or service meets the needs really important to them better than any competing drugs do.

- From any regulatory authorities, whether your drug is likely to meet the requirements of the regulatory authorities.

- From competitors, whether they are likely to be launching a competing drug in the near future.

Internally

- What is your operational capacity likely to be – and over time – from internal staff?

- What are levels of likely efficiency, operational flexibility and quality – again from internal staff?

- How high are unit cost levels – and how these will vary according to levels of activity – from financial spreadsheets and other estimations?

- What are the skills requirements in both quantity and cost – from human resources and operations?

At some point this data needs to be converted into cash flows, but this should wait until we have formulated the key assumptions which will underpin the pharma project.

ASSUMPTIONS EVALUATION

Defining the assumptions underpinning the value of the project requires considerable debate and challenge to provide a realistic basis for a business case. For example, if we go back to the new project in the earlier section on 'project definition' we might identify a number of key assumed cost value drivers. For instance, value drivers include:

- the new project adds superior customer value, enabling it to:

    - sustain volumes (of drug sales for existing customers);
    - increase margins (slightly);

- also, this enables new customers (or distribution channels) to be penetrated.

Cost drivers also include:

- the unit costs might be influenced by levels of activity through economies of scale;

- the cost of R&D processes, which is a key cost driver.

Here a 'value driver' can be defined as:

Anything either externally or internally within the business that might directly or indirectly generate positive cash inflows.

A 'cost driver' can be defined as:

Anything either externally or internally within the business that might directly or indirectly generate negative cash outflows.

Questions which help to test out the *external* assumptions for a pharma project are as follows, in the categories of:

- the competitive environment;

- customers and market trends.

These questions give managers checklists for evaluating any kind of pharma project.

Questions on the competitive environment (for externally-facing pharma projects) include:

1.   What assumptions about the competitive environment are implied by projected drug volumes, prices and margins, and how do these change over the life-cycle (for example, where the patent expires)?

2.   How might specific competitors be either addressing the same opportunity already or might they be able to respond quickly to your move (especially with generic drugs)?

Questions on customers and market trends include:

1.   How do customers (either distributors or patients) perceive the value of any end-product or service upon which the opportunity depends? (Consider, the perceived value of the drug – in their lives, or as a big therapeutic issue and so on.)

2.   How important is this value creation within the customer's own business value system, (for example the patient, the GP, the healthcare authority) and what interdependencies is this contingent upon?

EXERCISE – THE EXTERNAL EVALUATION OF A MAJOR PHARMACEUTICAL PROJECT

For one pharma project which you are currently considering doing, ask yourself:

- What do the checklists on the competitive environment and on customers/distributors and market trends tell you?
- What key questions now remain to be answered about these external aspects?
- How can you answer these questions with appropriate research within least time and cost?

To test the *internal* assumptions underpinning a pharma project we now suggest that the following questions are asked. These deal with investment, costs and implementation assumptions.

Investment-linked assumptions include:

1. What capacity levels are assumed (in drug processing)?

2. What unforeseen areas of investment may be required either of a future or indirect nature (for example, expansion of office space) not currently included in 'incremental' cashflows?

3. What hurdle rate of return is appropriate for this kind of pharma project?

The cost of capital will be more important where:

- cash inflows from investment decisions are relatively long term (particularly over five years hence);

- competitors might have access to cheaper sources of capital (for example, if they are based in Germany or Japan).

For pharma projects with shorter time horizons and paybacks, other issues – such as uncertainty, intangibles and interdependencies – will be probably much more important than calculating (and evaluating the value of) expected net cash flows over time.

Cost questions include:

1. How have 'incremental costs' been defined for the pharma project and how do cost apportionments incorporate a 'fair' allowance for direct and indirect resources absorbed by the activity?

2. What further R&D or other technical breakthroughs are assumed in order to support assumed levels of productivity?

3. What are the likely effects of reducing unit cost through gaining assumed economies of scale? Also, to what extent are unit costs increased if drug sales volumes are significantly less than 'most likely' assumptions?

Implementation assumptions include:

1.   Are timescales for implementation of the project realistic?

2.   Are there adequate operational resources to implement the project, especially where this relies upon scarce technical management and skills?

3.   Is the area of drug development or other area of advance and one where the pharma organisation (and key individuals) has both the capability, the commitment and, where relevant, the appropriate culture to make it a success?

4.   Who are the key stakeholders in the project, are they in favour, in neutral, or intangible, and what is their relative influence?

Once the key assumptions have been defined the next step is to begin to quantify the incremental cash flows associated with the project.

EXERCISE – THE INTERNAL EVALUATION OF A MAJOR PHARMACEUTICAL PROJECT

For the same pharma project (as you worked on earlier) that you are considering doing, ask yourself:

- What do the internal assumption checklists tell you about the durability of the project?
- What further data do you now need in order to formulate a robust business case?

ANALYSING IMPORTANCE AND UNCERTAINTY

Whilst the above illustration is a well worked through example of financial appraisal, it is only as good as the assumptions on which it is based.

One way of now testing the external and internal assumptions for the project is by using the Uncertainty–importance grid (derived from Mitroff and Linstone, 1993). Using this analysis grid (see Figure 5.4) managers can plot key assumptions driving the value of the pharma project decision. These can be external and internal, soft and hard assumptions.

An alternative format for this kind of analysis is the 'risk matrix' (see Figure 5.5). Here, the likelihood of success is on the horizontal axis, and is graded in three categories – likely, possible and remote. Also the vertical axis is the impact of success. This methodology is perhaps preferable where the project is not perhaps so likely to succeed. The uncertainty grid is perhaps superior when project success *is* likely, but you want to test its resilience.

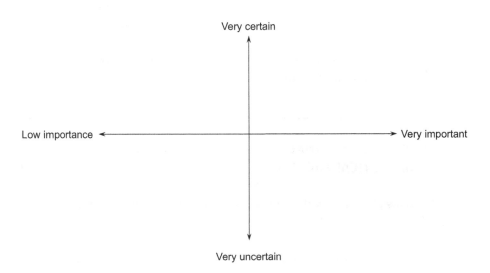

Figure 5.4   Uncertainy–importance grid

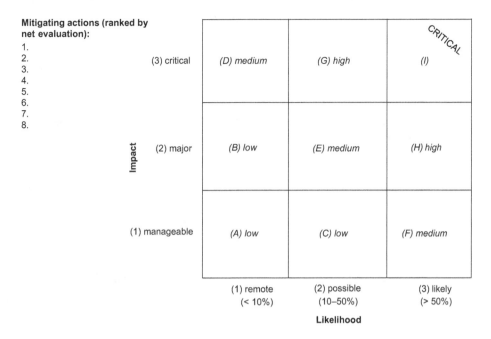

Figure 5.5   Risk matrix

Having selected a sub-set of these assumptions, these are now prioritised by using the grid. Once assumptions are carefully and skilfully defined, it is possible to debate the relative importance and uncertainty of these various assumptions, as we saw in Chapter 4.

At the beginning of the investment appraisal, key assumptions are likely to be mapped in the due north and north-east quadrants. Upon testing it is quite common to find one or more assumptions moving over to the danger zone in the south-east.

Figure 5.6 now actually relates to the new product launch in the following illustration. The extra sales volume from existing customers is very important, but also considered relatively certain. Sales to new customers are considerably more uncertain (but also very important) – shown in the south-east of the grid (Figure 5.6). Product launch costs are somewhat less important and also reasonably certain (shown just slightly north-east of the centre of the grid).

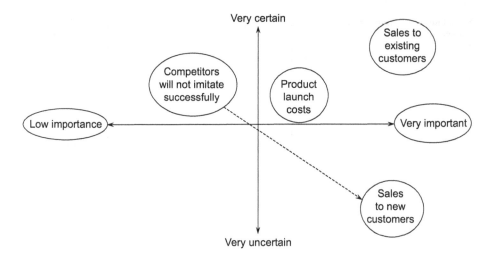

Figure 5.6   Uncertainty–importance grid: New product launch

In this illustration we refer to 'payback' which is defined as:

The period of time over which the initial project outlay is recouped.

In order to calculate the economic value of a pharma project, we need to examine its net cash flows; and to evaluate these using the company's cost of capital.

This proceeds in a number of steps:

1.   Ascertaining or defining the company's 'cost of capital' (based on input from Corporate Finance/Treasury).

2.   Estimating future net cash flows.

3.   Adjusting these to give a present (equivalent) value. This is done by discounting these future cash flows (that is, reducing their formula) to arrive at their 'net present value' (NPV) – the present value of future cash flows less the present value of all outlays.

4.   Performing a sensitivity analysis of this NPV (following on from the uncertainty analysis conducted earlier).

The 'cost of capital' is usually the weighted coverage of the company's cost of risk capital and the cost of its debt.

Outlays occur in the drug development stages (in drug discovery, pre-clinical, clinical trials and registration).

Net (positive) operating cash flows begin around year 13 and continue through to year 20 at (hopefully) a high level – to the end of the drug's patent life and beyond. The bulk of outlays occur in phase III, during expensive clinical trials, when typically around 40 per cent of the cost of the drug research and development is incurred (through clinical trials).

Table 5.1 gives us much simplified and fictitious illustration of a drug's NPV. We have included (at year 20) a 'terminal value' of US$40m to cover the present value (at that stage) of the drugs net revenues – based on it now having become a generic drug. (A NPV is defined as being the present value of the cash inflows of the project, minus the present value of the outlays.)

The particular cash flow profile in the example gives on NPV of US$122, which is a healthy return over-and-above the cost of capital. Given the risks inherent in the drug development and launch process this is not an unfairly generous level of returns. (For more on defining the cost of capital, which is beyond the scope of this book, see Grundy, 2002).

For simplicity, in Table 5.1, we have shown not just the costs of developing one drug (in the early stages), but of many. For each successful drug a considerable number of compounds may need to be developed (to the clinical trials phase).

Table 5.1   An example of a financial appraisal of a new drug

Years	R&D Investment US$m	Operating Cash flows* US$m	Terminal value US$m	Net cash flows US$m	Present value** US$m
1	(30)			(30)	(26)
2	(35)			(35)	(28)
3	(40)			(40)	(28)
4	(40)			(40)	(25)
5	(90)			(90)	(51)
6	(110)			(110)	(55)
7	(25)			(25)	(11)
8	(25)			(25)	(10)
9	(30)			(30)	(10)
10	(25)			(25)	(8)
11	(25)			(25)	(7)
12	(25)			(25)	(6)
13		350		350	70
14		350		350	62
15		350		350	54
16		350		350	49
17		350		350	44
18		350		350	39
19		350		350	35
20		350	40	390	34
Total	(500m)	2800	40	2340	122

NPV is US$ 122 million or US$ 388 million less US$266 million.

*   Sales less operating costs.

**   Assumed weighted average cost of capital of 12 per cent.

As an alternative methodology, one might include in the computation *only* the drug development costs of a single compound. But we would then multiply future net cash flows from the drug by a probability factor, of say 5 or 10 per cent, to reflect the lack of certainty that it would be successful. A simple example of this would be (with a 5 per cent chance of ultimate success, and net revenues in year x of (US$100 million):

$$\textit{Expected future value} \quad = 5\% \times US\$100m$$
$$= US\$5m$$

Clearly, to the extent that not all drugs will pass clinical tests and also might not clear regulatory hurdles, then again an 'expected value' based on a probability × net cash flows should be used. The following points are interesting in Table 5.1:

- Whilst the projects' cash inflows appear to be considerable when each period is divided by a compounded annual factor of 1.12 (to reflect the weighted average cost of capital), the present value shrinks considerably.

- So too does the present value of outlays, to about half of the actual cash outlays: but the discounting effect of the cash flows in years 13 to 20 is that bit more harsh.

- The present value from generic drugs (following year 20) is very minor, (a) because of lower margins, but (b) because it is so far into the future.

- Should the project be delayed this may have a very big impact on NPV, (a) because you have less time before the patent expires, and (b) because cash inflows are pushed out into the future.

With regard to the final bullet point above it is possible (using the above calculations) to show how much a delay of a month, or even a delay with cost in terms of NPV cost. It is well known in the industry that these costs are large, and yet often project plans are unrealistic and get changed with an inevitably disruptive effect. These cash profiles are thus very closely parallel to Figure 5.7, sharing cash being recouped later on in the life of a drug.

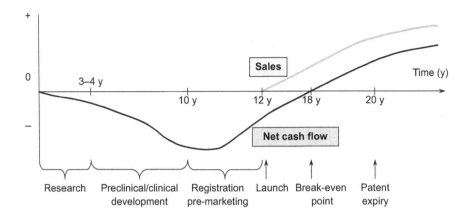

Figure 5.7   Net cash flow and sales in the pharmaceutical industry

UNDERSTANDING THE DYNAMICS OF UNCERTAINTY – AND OF SCENARIOS

Here the Uncertainty–importance grid needs to be accompanied by some intensive thinking about the system which drives key uncertainties for any major pharma project. This can be represented as the uncertainty tunnel (see Figure 5.8). The uncertainty tunnel is depicted as a tunnel bounded by constraints on what is possible within a project's environment. Essentially, uncertainty is seen as driven by unpredictable change.

In Figure 5.8 unpredictable change is explored by looking at its precursors (that is, what has affected the project previously from its environment). Pharma managers analyse these factors either amplifying or dampening a particular unpredictable change.

Following this analysis we then examine the immediate versus the longer-term consequences of change on the project, perhaps discriminating between its first, second and third order consequences.

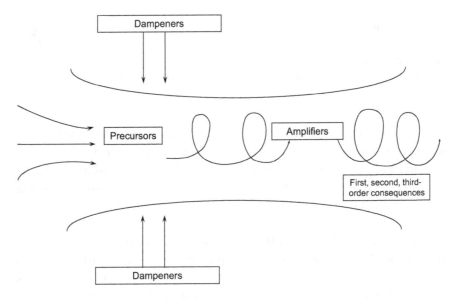

Figure 5.8   The uncertainty tunnel

EXERCISE – USING THE UNCERTAINTY TUNNEL MODEL

For one project that you are contemplating, ask yourself:

- What are the precursors to the project?
- What factors might amplify uncertainty?
- What factors might dampen uncertainty?
- What are the potential first, second and third order consequences of a shift in the project's internal or external environment? (Allow yourself to tell scenario stories at this point.)

Besides scenarios and more qualitative uncertainty analysis, a number of other methodologies have been used over the years to cope with evaluating uncertainty.

Forcasting the outcomes of drug development is a difficult process – and whilst estimates of drug's economic value (or NPV) can be done on a spreadsheet, such single value assessments are unlikely to actually occur.

Numerical methods that are known as 'Monte Carlo' methods can be used to look at the probabilities of possible outcomes on a computer. These are statistical simulation methods that utilise sequences of random numbers to perform a simulation. The name 'Monte Carlo' was coined because of similarities with the game of chance in a casino.

When we use the word *simulation*, we refer to any analytical method meant to imitate a real-life system, especially when other analyses are too mathematically complex or too difficult to reproduce. A Monte Carlo simulation randomly generates values for certain variables and then uses decision-tree methodology (see below) to simulate a model of expected results.

For each uncertain variable the range and frequency distribution is defined. The simulation calculates multiple scenarios of a model by repeating sampling values from probability distributions for the uncertain variables and using those values for the cell. Simulations can consist of as many trials (or scenarios) as you want – hundreds or even thousands – in just a few seconds. In drug development some of the key uncertain variables which can be simulated using Monte Carlo methods are:

- drug efficiency;

- costs of drug developing;

- time to market;

- penetration of market;

- drug price.

Monte Carlo methods are increasingly in use in the pharma industry as a way of coping with uncertainty and risk, and in making trade-offs between the various controllable variables.

Unfortunately, Monte Carlo methods are complicated and require sophisticated skills in interpreting distributions of possible results – they are not for the faint-hearted!

More specifically, decision trees can be used to explore the possible sequences of events which might occur within a project. Probabilities are then attached to each possibility. The 'expected value' (or the probability of the event-multiplied by its pay-off) is then calculated. Decision-tree analysis is used quite frequently in the 'go/no-go' drug development decision-making process. This can be worked through by working backwards using feasibility analysis, for example of:

- toxicity being highlighted from chemical structure (for example, oncogenicity);

- achieving the defined, unique, selling propositions;

- a commercially acceptable cost of goods;

- sufficient bioavailability for oral application;

- once daily application if required for marketing reasons; and

- a sufficient stable formulation.

Eventually, one then arrives at a present, expected (economic) value for the project.

Figure 5.9 shows a decision tree for a pharma alliance. Alliances are particularly uncertain – due to a combination of market operational and political uncertainties. The decision-tree approach is thus particularly well suited to this area of application.

Figure 5.10 shows a typical decision tree for drug development and also one for business development generally. The advantage of a decision-tree approach based on pure expected value is also simplicity. Its disadvantage is that it does not cope well where there is not a normal distribution curve of outcomes. So whilst one might have one expected value, the reality might be that in most situations the result is either much better or worse.

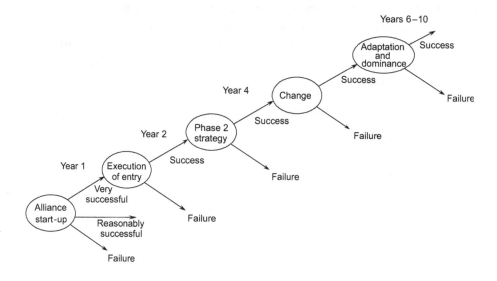

Figure 5.9   Decision tree

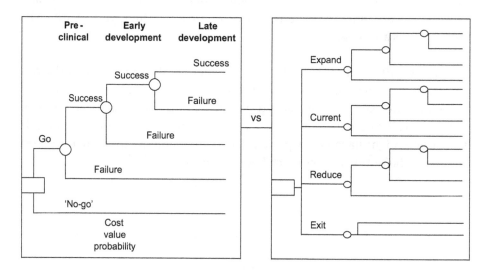

Figure 5.10   Portfolio management: Decision trees

Another way of looking at risks and uncertainty often used in the pharma industry is to look at how the probability of success changes as the various stages of drug development are completed (see Figure 5.11). This can be used also to help target improvements in project success rate through innovative methodology. As a result of the changes in the industry, due to adverse environmental shift (economic and regulatory) and the difficulty of getting the same effect from blockbusters, it is likely that the projected NPVs of drug development projects will be lower in the future than in the past. Also, there will be a lot more attention to risk management – reinforcing the importance of tools like decision trees.

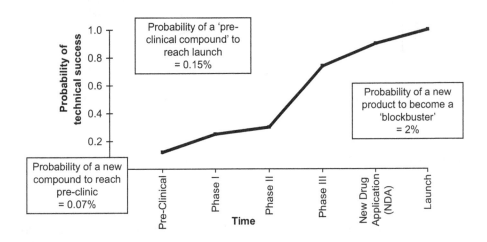

Figure 5.11   Risks in the drug development process

Exploring the 'Do-Nothing' Or Base Case

Before we leave the topic of assumptions for the pharma project we also need to explore the 'do-nothing' or base case option (Grundy, 1998a).

The base case is what might happen without the investment decision. Traditional financial theory teaches us to evaluate incremental cashflows, 'incremental' meaning the difference between net cash flows both with and without the investment project.

A major problem with the base case is that of predicting the rate or pace of decline. This is inherently difficult to predict. Some managers may then try to shield financially suspect projects behind the argument that unless the project is implemented, the strategic and financial health of the business will be irreparably damaged. See Figure 5.12 for a classic illustration of a declining base case.

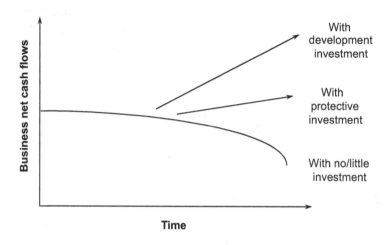

Figure 5.12   The effects of the declining base case

The important thing to remember with the base case is that you need to spend almost as much time thinking about the world in which one does not do the investment as the world in which one does.

EXERCISE – EVALUATING THE BASE CASE FOR A PHARMACEUTICAL PROJECT

For a project where, in a 'do-nothing' situation the business revenues are in decline, ask yourself:

- What is the likely pace of decline?
- What might accelerate this pace of decline?
- What other measures (other than incremental investment) might mitigate the decline?
- Is the decline sufficiently cataclysmic to suggest that it may even be worthwhile exiting this business rather than investing more in it?

Returning briefly to the AID grid from Chapter 4, there are interesting implications of doing versus not doing the pharma project. Figure 5.12 shows the 'with the project case' as only marginally attractive, and also as relatively difficult. But the 'without the project case', the business is actually in decline (and thus has negative attractiveness), and is very difficult.

Thus although going ahead with the project does not look particularly wonderful on a 'with the project case' only, considering the negative base case that is avoided, it actually does become attractive. The value of this kind of project is thus *protective* rather than offensive.

These characterisations of value are just two of many possible examples of how to segment projects. For example, projects can have an 'opportunity' value in opening up doorways to future value. Or, they might have a 'synergistic' value along with other projects. They might also be of 'sweat' value, simply squeezing more out of the same or out of less resource. Finally, they may be of 'deliberate' or 'emergent' value, emergent value being value which was not actually anticipated but which came out of unexpected alignment.

Intangibles and Interdependencies

With regard to intangibles, pharma projects add value only in so far as they are part of the business value system. Interdependencies thus need to be explored because they are essential in understanding how the business operates as a total competitive and financial system.

INTERDEPENDENCIES

Interdependencies exist in a variety of forms. Some interdependencies are external and reflect the impact of one external assumption on one another. For example, a resurgence of economic growth may increase the size of a particular market and also attract in new entrants.

Many of the internal assumptions depend upon external variables, giving rise to even more interdependencies (for instance, competitive rivalry may lead to a high incidence of price discounting and thus to lower margins).

But many of the more interesting interdependencies are those within the architecture of the business strategy itself. For instance, one product may benefit or suffer due to the introduction of a new product.

The analysis of interdependencies should follow on from the analysis and testing of the external and internal assumptions. Where the decision process is of a less formal nature analysing interdependencies should be integral with the evaluation of assumptions.

EXERCISE – INTERDEPENDENCIES OF A PHARMACEUTICAL PROJECT

For one major project of your choice, ask yourself:

- What are the key interdependencies between this project and other projects within the business, or other business activities generally?
- What interdependencies are both most important and uncertain? (You may wish to use the Uncertainty–importance grid at this point)
- What would you need to do to align these interdependencies, and what might this cost?

INTANGIBLES

Intangibles are one of the main curses of project appraisal. For many managers, intangibles have become the 'no-go' zone of financial analysis. Although these areas of value are extremely difficult to quantify in financial terms (and perhaps impossible to quantify with precision), there are invariably ways of defining intangibles better. This can be done by looking at the project from different perspectives:

- Competitive: The impact on patient or other customer perceptions of value or in measurable improvement vis-à-vis competitors.

- Operational: Performance improvement or flexibility of operations.

- Organisational: Impact on morale and, indirectly, on motivation.

- Opportunity generation: The opportunity which might be opened up or explored as a result of the investment project.

The first step with intangibles is to ask 'why is the value thought to be of an intangible nature?' This may be because:

- The benefit accrues to the drug distributor or to the patient rather than directly to the company (either the patent or the channel to market). However, there may also be indirect benefits to the company via reducing the chances of the drug distributor switching to another competing therapeutic treatment or through increasing the price of the drug, or through protection against the discounting associated with the commodity, generic drugs. (This might take the form of a project to increase marketing spend on a generic drug whose patent has just expired.)

- The benefit accrues via a number of internal interdependencies with other areas of the business, or these may occur because the project is essentially part of the 'business' infrastructure.

- The benefit comes due to the project being essentially protective or defensive in nature.

A process for dealing with intangibles is therefore:

- To identify *why* the value is of an intangible nature.

- To seek *possible alternative measures* to help target and provide indicators of alternative measures to those of purely financial value (see Table 5.2).

- Through *management consensus,* to compare what value managers are prepared to put on the intangible (this is sometimes called the 'Delphi' approach – as in the famous Greek oracle).

An example of managing intangibles can be drawn from ICI Biosciences (which our case study in Chapter 1). A number of acquisitions of existing companies had been made, with ICI Biosciences paying significant sums for 'goodwill'. These businesses were held at the time to have considerable intangible value, particularly:

- through providing the platform to exploit new breakthroughs in genetic technology (but what was the likelihood of this breakthrough, how would ICI capture its value in the market place – using these companies, and for how long?);

- by achieving operational synergies with the other newly acquired companies (but *who* would harvest these synergies, *how* and *when*?).

In the event, these intangibles proved elusive for ICI Biosciences, the moral being: do not hide behind the difficulties of evaluating the intangibles.

Table 5.2   Types of intangibles and possible measures

Types of intangibles	Related to other appraisal problems	Possible focus for measurement
Drug image	Evaluating value to intermediate/ end customers	Patients' views of product
Reduced customer product and service	Evaluating value to intermediate/ end customers	Patients' views of costs and risks
Patient loyalty	Evaluating value to intermediate/ end customers	Estimated revenue and likelihood of distributors switching
Protection of your business	Protective value	Monitoring incidence of existing loss of business
Spin-off opportunity, for example, future drug development	Contingent value and interdependency	Specify conditions under which the opportunity may arise and is harvested
Flexibility	External and internal interdependency	Specify the conditions under which flexibility will add value
Cost savings elsewhere	Internal interdependency	Before and after measurement of cost drivers and their impact
Alignment of both external and internal factors	External and internal interdependency	Specification of the conditions under which alignment may occur and probable value

---

EXERCISE – INTANGIBLES

For one or more area of intangibles, in your pharma project, use Table 5.2 to examine the basis of their value and ask yourself:

- What is the underlying nature of this particular intangible?
- How might it be measured (or how might its key indicators be monitored)?
- Ultimately, if its full potential for cash generation is realised (both directly and indirectly), what might its value be worth?

We now develop a series of decision rules for managing intangibles. This takes us through the following stages:

- Why is the value intangible, for example:

    - Is it future and contingent?
    - Is it generated by value-sharing, for example, with customers?
    - Is it protective value?
    - Is it created by synergies within the pharma business value system?

- How is it created?

- When will it be created?

- How will it be captured?

- And by whom?

- How much value will be created, and at what cost?

Business Case

We now examine what should now be in a business case for a pharma project. When someone says the words 'business case', managers often think of a weighty, detailed document with lots of hard facts and financial numbers. But the real point of a business case is to gain more clarity about the objectives of the pharma project, its implications for the business and particularly to expose and test the key assumptions which drive value. This can be achieved in a very succinct way, by for instance restricting the business case to a maximum of eight pages, as described below (often less will suffice).

SUGGESTED FORMAT FOR A BUSINESS CASE FOR A PHARMA PROJECT

- Executive summary (1 page);

- project definition, objectives and scope (1 page);

- how the project adds value (new opportunity, tangible synergy, defensive or protective value) (1 page);

- key external and internal assumptions (with an evaluation of importance and uncertainty) (3 pages);

- implementation issues (1 page);

- summary financials (1 page).

This brings the length to eight pages, plus detailed appendices containing technical issues, market projecting distribution issues, technical details, detailed financial and non-financial measures and milestones, detailed financial sensitivities, and detailed resource requirements – possibly another seven pages. This brings a typical case to just 15 pages, assuming that you can write succinctly!

EXERCISE – THE PHARMACEUTICAL BUSINESS CASE

Using the above format for a business case for an existing pharma project proposal, ask yourself:

- What key questions remain to be answered about the value of the pharma project?
- What data do you now need to answer these questions (and at least cost)?
- What process of management reflection, learning and review would now help to refine a most robust but realistic business case?

CONSTRUCTING A BUSINESS CASE

Below are some practical tips on putting together a robust business case for a pharma project:

- Involve a good spread of managers and technical advisers – and from a range of disciplines in project definition, option generation and data collection in a targeted way. This will ensure your assumptions get a good reality check, and that you identify a good range of options; and also the key implementation constraints, and begin to position your project for endorsement.

- Be disciplined in your data collection: only collect data which will help you make the critical assumptions which the project depends on. (This actually means spending less time on those assumptions which are less critical, such as more minor, internal overhead costs).

- Integrate the data in a preliminary workshop to evaluate options and assumptions in a creative way (do not lose focus in a series of meetings spread over time).

- Take the point of view of other stakeholders in the organisation. Consider which assumptions are *most important to them* and where will their judgements differ from yours, and why. Experiment here with the 'out-of-body' experience – imagine you actually are that stakeholders – what attracts you towards or repels you away from the project?

- Do not try to obscure or conceal the project's downsides. An astute review panel will quickly identify issues which you have glossed over. Your 'out-of-body' simulation will equip you to have a balanced debate on the merits of the project.

Business cases will therefore only add value therefore if:

- they are clear, succinct, and written in a jargon-free style;

- they expose the most important and uncertain assumptions, and also address these both in the sensitivity analysis and via contingency planning;

- they do not fall into the trap of seeing the financial numbers as absolute measures of value, but use these creatively. For instance, in dealing with less tangibles it may be fruitful to put an illustrative value on 'what might these be worth?' so that a more balanced, overall appraisal of the project can be achieved.

We have argued throughout the need to understand the key value drivers and to expose and challenge the key assumptions *before* undertaking the sensitivity analysis. 'Better practice' means doing very rigorous testing of those key variables which are likely to be most uncertain and most important.

It is only by working this way around that true sensitivity analysis is performed, otherwise all you may end up with is 'insensitivity analysis' – playing with the assumption-set to get an acceptable answer – a positive NPV (which in this case means no more than 'numbers prevent vision').

Portfolio Management

'Portfolio management' can be defined as the systematic comparison of projects against two or more decision-making criteria. Portfolio management (see Figure 5.13) is the interface between R&D strategies and specific projects.

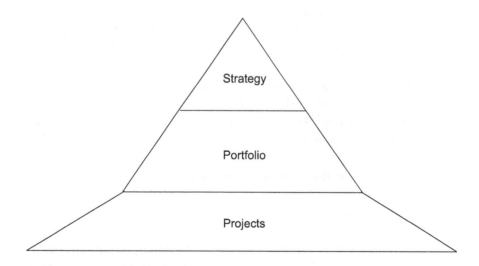

Figure 5.13   R&D management

We have already considered a number of techniques for portfolio management. These include:

- the project option grid;

- the attractiveness-implementation difficulty grid (or 'AID' analysis);

- 'economic attractiveness' versus 'feasibility' – as criteria.

In addition, it may also be useful to rate projects against their likely return, versus risk. This could be done by using Figure 5.14.

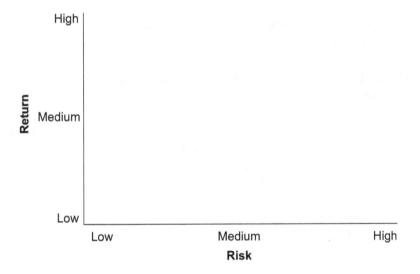

Figure 5.14   Return versus risk

The objectives of portfolio management are:

- to get highest and the best use of each project;

- to allocate resources wisely;

- to select the right projects to achieve R&D and business objectives;

- to find a rational for prioritisation;

- to gain commitment of organisation.

Portfolio management:

- is needed in order to cope with multiple opportunities, limited resources, continual change and uncertainty – and differing time horizons;

- is used to identify the gap(s) between the current portfolio and overall strategic goals, besides setting priorities and also resource allocation;

- is used to estimate both the economic value of the overall portfolio and of specific projects;

- can be used as a decision both to decide to rationalise a drug product portfolio.

Besides AID analysis (used for judging internal criteria), the criteria of 'strategic attractiveness' can be broken down into: product/market attractiveness, and competitive position (see Figure 5.15).

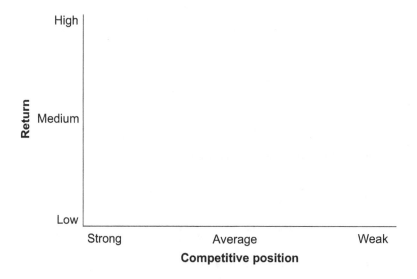

Figure 5.15   Attractiveness/postioning grid

In the pharma industry one would normally then brake 'product/market attractions' into:

- the attractiveness of the specific biology;

- the relative importance of the therapy in patient's lives;

- the availability and relative efficacy of substitutes.

'Competitive position' can also be broken down into:

- drug efficacy;

- mode lease of treatment;

- existence and severity of size of side-effects;

- likely market share;

- branding;

- ready availability of suitable distribution channels.

In conclusion, besides financial and probability analysis, portfolio analysis plays a very important role in evaluating pharma projects.

Conclusion

Project evaluation for pharma projects is not just a matter of number-crunching some cash flows in order to justify investment in the project. It is a very thorough testing, and in many cases a re-formulation of the project strategy – and perhaps even of its scope and main focus.

Project evaluation brings together analysis of both the external and internal pharma environment (and assumptions about that environment) – and translates this picture into value- and cost-driver analysis. Only when this is done is it feasible to begin a more detailed financial appraisal.

Pharmaceutical Project Mobilisation, Control and Learning

Introduction

In this chapter we look at the steps needed to flesh out implementation plans for pharma projects and how they can be monitored more effectively in the following areas:

- project mobilisation and roles;

- project milestones and indicators;

- project systems;

- project learning;

- project dynamics.

The 'project milestones and indicators' includes a number of helpful figures to will enable you to monitor pharma projects more effectively.

Project Mobilisation and Roles

Diagnosing a pharma project, defining its strategy and evolving a project plan are merely the precursors of actually beginning a project. But unfortunately many managers get caught up in the reflective mode of strategic or tactical thought and become incapable of taking the first steps into action. Just like the American hero in the film *Baby Steps*, who became a guru by encouraging people just to take the very first step towards the goal – however distant – just making the very first step in a project will, given a robust strategy, probably take you, in effect, a third to a half-way to its completion.

Mobilisation implies some degree of commitment – and that potentially means some exposure to risk. Even if the first steps are taken in a project then energy can quickly dissipate. Continual management and monitoring of the energy is required. Alongside the energy exhibited by the project team we can begin to draw curves over time, particularly of:

- energy over time (see Figure 6.1);

- commitment over time (see Figure 6.2).

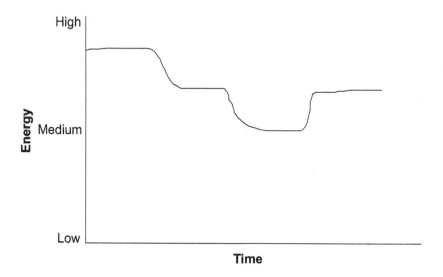

Figure 6.1   Energy over time curve

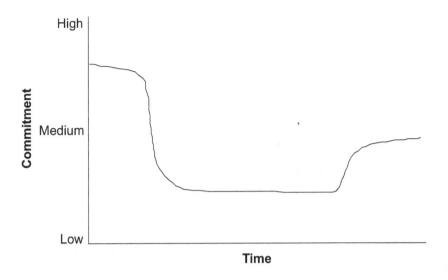

Figure 6.2   Commitment over time curve

By anticipating and monitoring these variables over time it is possible to gain a greater influence over the softer aspects of the pharma project management process.

The curves in Figures 6.1 and 6.2 can be used for a variety of purposes, particularly:

- to anticipate future energy and commitment within the pharma project;

- to monitor where the project is now;

- to reflect upon (and learn from) past experience of the pharma project.

Interestingly, one group of managers in the pharma industry found it very difficult to maintain the energy level in a project team as their everyday activity involved moving from one project to the next incessantly. The consequence of this was that they hardly had any energy at all, which gave a good indication of their process!

Project roles are equally vital in securing the achievement of milestones. For each milestone the project plan needs to specify who will be delivering it. This may fruitfully distinguish between the individual(s) who is actually going to ensure that project activity has delivered it versus those who have provided an input to the process. It may also distinguish (in organisational terms) between:

- the end-users (of the project);

- the project team and its leader;

- the project sponsor.

An obvious point, but one which needs spelling out nevertheless, is that roles should be allocated not to who happens to be available to the project but only to those who *fit* project roles. Too often people get allocated a project who happen to be 'around' but who either lack the technical, managerial or political skills, or the appropriate management style to really make the project a success.

For very major pharma projects it is imperative to get a Board of Directors sponsor, , otherwise the project may lack appropriate positioning in the organisation or may lack a sufficient power (and influence) base.

The sponsor must not be someone who regards this role as an ornamental responsibility. They must have a genuine passion for the project – and be visibly active in championing its cause.

Project Milestones and Indicators

Milestones form the key methodology for project control. A project milestone can be defined as being:

The time by which some specific project deliverable has been achieved.

When planning a pharma project one normally works backwards from the milestones to the present, rather than vice versa. This means that you are less inclined to indulge in spurious or dilutive activity.

Sadly, many managers become overly preoccupied by project milestones and neglect the 'how' of the project: its strategy and plan. These are crucial and to some extent are more important than the project milestones themselves. Remember that the whole point of a project is to achieve the result in least time and cost.

EXERCISE – MILESTONES

For one pharma project, which you are currently managing, ask yourself:

- What are the milestones for each key stage (or activity) of the project?
- Do these milestones actually specify both the quantitative and quantitative aspects of key deliverables?
- Is this sufficiently clear so that an alien (as it were) could understand it and thus know what was expected out of the project (and by when)?

Figures 6.3 to 6.12 provide you with some useful tabular formats for project planning and control. Figure 6.3 is a high level document for the Project Plan, whilst Figure 6.4 gives a breakdown of resources, assumptions, independencies and constraints.

Project scope and timescale	Project sponsor:
Key objectives 1. 2. 3. 4. Scope considerations 1. 2 3.	Project manager: Project team key members: Other key stakeholders:

Figure 6.3   Project plan

Key enablers	Key resources
Key constraints	Key assumptions (most important and uncertainty)
Key interdependencies	Project financial value (approximately)

Figure 6.4   Project plan: Resources, assumptions, interdependencies and constraints

Key activity	Key milestones	Key person(s) responsible

Figure 6.5   Project plan: Key activities and milestones

Figure 6.5 then breaks the project down into activities, milestones and responsibilities.

Figure 6.6 looks at your communication plan and Figure 6.7 your organisation plan. More specifically Figure 6.8 is a detailed breakdown for a clinical trial milestones schedule.

Communication plan (date:)					
Name and job title/position	Contact details Tel./email/fax. Address location	What do they need to know and level of detail and frequently?	What information do you need from them and how frequently?	How important are they to the project?	What meetings do they need to attend?

Figure 6.6   Project plan: Communication plan

Project organisation chart (date updated:)						
Name and job title/position	Contact details Tel./email/fax Address location	Best time of day and preferred communica-tion media	Name of line manager	Name of contact person if not available	Internal or external to the company	Distribution lists on/ information need to provide

Figure 6.7   Project plan: Organisation chart

Milestone	Due date	Revised date	Actual date
Study budget approved			
Investigator brochure finalised			
Protocol finalised			
CRF finalised			
Study drug available			
Ethics approval			
Regulatory approval			
First patient in			
Last patient in			
Last patient out			
Statistical analysis plan			
Database lock			
Final report			
Publication manuscript submitted			
Publication date			

Figure 6.8   Project plan: Clinical trial milestones schedule

Finally, Figure 6.9, 6.10 and 6.11 cover formats for progress monitoring, and 6.12 is a format for project meetings.

Progress Monitor Report						
Project						
Report prepared by:				Date of report:		
Task no.	Task description	Planned		Actual		Expected duration
		Start	Finish	Start	Finish	
15	Prepare protocol	12 Jan	12 Feb			
17	Select investigators	20 Jan	1 Mar			
22	Organise monitors meeting	15 Feb	15 Mar			

Figure 6.9   Progress monitor report

Progress Monitor Report: Outstanding Issues					
Project					
Report prepared by:				Date of report:	
Task no.	Task Description	Issue	Proposed solution(s)	Resolution date	
				Planned	Actual

Figure 6.10   Progress monitor report: Outstanding issues

Progress Monitor Report: Outstanding issues continued	
Project	
Report prepared by:	Date of report:
Problems encountered	
Technical difficulties	
Problems anticipated with activities still to be carried out or in progress	

Figure 6.11   Progress monitor report: Outstanding issues continued

Action Meeting List		**Date of meeting:**		
		Prepared by:		
Present		**Absent**		
Actions from last meeting still outstanding				
Action	Person responsible	Planned date	Date	
			Revised	Actual
Actions from current meeting				

Figure 6.12   Action meeting list

Where a pharma project fails to achieve its designated milestone, then the next step is, unsurprisingly, to do a fishbone analysis of the root cause of its failure.

Besides specific project milestones for certain projects (like change management) where it is harder to define more specific milestones, it is as well to also specify some key indicators. Key indicators are some of the softer and more qualitative deliverables of the project. So, for example, with a culture change project in the pharma industry (for instance following a merger) we would need to examine each of the key shifts which were the goal of the project and then ask the question:

What are the key indicators for this shift to have actually occurred?

A guiding principle overall is to ensure that project milestones and indicators do not become a bureaucracy. Their whole purpose is to energise, mobilise and focus, not to become ends in themselves.

Project Systems

IT systems play an increasingly important role in supporting effective project management in the pharma industry. The most obvious application is to project planning. In particular, Microsoft Project has transformed the way in which activities and their critical paths can be managed ahead – and in the context of changing circumstances and assumptions. Microsoft Project is still the preferred project management software used by pharma organizations, and can be tailored to meet their specific needs.

Whilst such systems may be wonderful in helping to produce detailed plans, they can encourage pharma managers to become over-concerned with getting to an *accurate* assessment of project lead-time – whilst not necessarily being realistic – given the inherent uncertainties and imponderables surrounding the project.

Besides project planning and decision-support systems, there are increasing requirements to store data on projects. This is both for internal, technical purposes, and also to comply with regulatory requirements for clinical research projects. Again, IT solutions have made dramatic improvements to how these complex and costly requirements can be managed. We now illustrate an even more novel application – using IT to help make drug development decisions.

Our first case study is on the topic of decision-support systems. In it, Clinical Discovery's systems for deciding which compounds to test in the 'Discovery' phase are explored.

CASE EXAMPLE – DECISION SUPPORT AND CLINICAL DISCOVERY

The past decade has seen pharma companies spending increasing sums of money to fill their drug development pipeline. However, for the most part these efforts have been unsuccessful '(Despite Billions for Discoveries, Pipeline of Drugs Is Far From Full' *New York Times*, 19 April, 2002). One of the key obstacles to an efficient pipeline is selecting the right compound from among the many available. This necessitates improvements in the process of pharma companies, which is explained in the following case study of a major pharma company.

Clinical Discovery Inc. (CDI) has developed a modelling and simulation platform that enables pharma companies to blend medical, pharmacological and other expertise with data analysis and statistics, deriving useful information from complex clinical data sets. CDI was approached by a large pharma company with the challenge of assisting it in deciding which compound from among close to 100 to test in humans. Despite laboratory and animal studies the pharma company's experts still were unsure with which drug to proceed – a critical decision point in their drug development. We will not go into detail describing CDI's technology (www.clinicald.com) but will focus instead on the conclusions reached during the course of this project.

The drug candidates, starting with a base compound, were synthesised using specific chemical structures known to have effects on a particular neurological disease. Once synthesised, the basic compound, together with variants, underwent in-vitro testing in the sponsor's laboratories. Inhibitory concentrations were derived from an appropriate medium that served as a surrogate for the animal model.

Based on these values, most compounds were discarded (a decision point), and those remaining were promoted to in-vivo testing. The in-vivo test phase included assessing the compound's LD50 and ED50 values of which more than one effect was evaluated. Non-lethal side-effects were then assessed, and three categories of adverse events were evaluated. Based on the in-vivo testing, decisions were made as to which compound would advance to phase I trials (another decision point). The pharma company provided CDI with its in-vitro and in-vivo results. In addition, CDI's analysts were given the company's experts' weighting of these factors, enabling them to answer the question, 'How important is this specific factor?'

CDI's methodology and technology captures the overall approach to the development process as illustrated by a KnowledgeTree™ created for this study (see Figure 6.13). CDI's modelers merged the KnowledgeTree™ with test metrics to generate models for the two previously mentioned decision points.

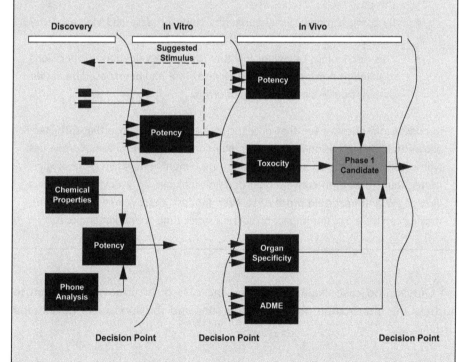

Figure 6.13   Clinical discovery decision tree for drug development case study

Below are several interesting findings that can be applied generally to pharma projects:

- CDI's methodology established that in-vivo results are predictable from the in-vitro results.
- The necessary data to support such modelling is already available and under the control of the pharma company – yet not being properly exploited.
- Modelling showed that poor decisions had been made previously. Some compounds were inappropriately discarded, while others that were bound to fail were inappropriately promoted to the in-vivo stage. This resulted in lost time, wasted money, and delays in reaching the clinical trial stage and market, thereafter.
- Modellers and analysts can capture and systematise the decision-making process and identify the weights and factors most critical to this process.
- By using a model, likely variations could be assessed via sensitivity analysis.
- This technology allowed for the rapid re-evaluation of decisions reached at previous stages in the study that had been based on earlier assumptions – a major source of errors.

In conclusion, one can see that new techniques, such as those that CDI used, allowed for better decision-making. To remain competitive, the pharma companies will increasingly have to select and then implement innovative technologies, rather than relying on conventional decision-making. Drug development is a very costly and uncertain process: so even modest improvements in decision-making can have a major impact on success rates, time-to market and cost.

Our second case example looks at the case of an innovative system to address the information needs of study sites and the sponsor in developing drugs.

CASE EXAMPLE – GLASER PEDIATRIC RESEARCH

The following interview was conducted in February 2003 with Ms. Karen Urbanek, Research Program Manager, Glaser Pediatric Research Network, Palo Alto, California. The Glaser Pediatric Research Network is an innovative collaborative network, linking world-class scientific centers of excellence with the latest technology to catalyse rapid progress on serious and life-threatening pediatric illnesses. The Glaser Pediatric Research Network is comprised of:

- Texas Children's Hospital, Baylor College of Medicine;
- Children's Hospital, Boston and Harvard Medical School;
- Lucille Packard Children's Hospital, Stanford University School of Medicine;
- Mattel Children's Hospital, University of California at Los Angeles;
- Children's Medical Center, University of California at San Francisco.

Velos eResearch is an Internet service and software product provided by Velos Inc. (www.veloseresearch.com) that addresses the information needs of clinical investigators and their sponsors. It provide a comprehensive project management system designed to help study sites project manage their clinical research activities, and also to improve communication between sites and sponsor. The project management facilities which can be used include the following:

- building online protocols;
- tracking amendments and approvals;
- sharing protocols with other select users;
- using customisable templates to create standardised protocols; generating online and printed reports;
- using Wizards to generate intelligent calendars that automate the creation of trial schedules for patients;
- accessing a reusable protocol library to reduce the work involved in the design process and allows visits to be mapped to associated costs, resources, forms and messages.

Also available is access to online management of patients and study processes such as design, Institutional Review Board (IRB) approvals, scheduling and project management. The Patient Tracking module allows accounts to incorporate capabilities such as adverse event tracking, CRF status tracking and enhanced scheduling.

In this interview, Ms Urbanek speaks of her excitement about Velos eResearch. The Glaser Pediatric Research Network was planning to launch its first study in April 2003).

Velos: What are the major value additions you expect the Velos system to deliver?

Ms Urbanek: What excites me most about Velos eResearch is that it can be used to manage several, concurrent, multi-site studies in areas such as coordination of study documents and patient scheduling. The Events Library should be helpful for supporting future and concurrent protocols where tests and assessments overlap.

Velos: What do you expect to change or improve most in your day-to-day operations?

Ms Urbanek: Research networks often have a tough time sharing their documents and protocols. Investigators often have different versions of the protocols, making coordination and collaboration difficult. My hope is to improve quality and efficiency since Velos eResearch is an Internet solution. With Velos eResearch, we plan to maintain our documents on the Internet, so that everyone is on the same page.

From an efficiency perspective, the Event Library should be useful as we will have similar tasks and assessments across studies. We could pull up previously defined events from the Library and use them again as we progress through new studies.

Velos: What are some of the challenges you might expect in 'rolling out' Velos?

Ms Urbanek: One challenge is that with web-based systems, some people perceive that there is a security issue and sponsors might be hesitant to put their information out on the web, or store confidential patient information on the web, no matter how secure it might truly be.

Velos: Is security an issue for you?

Ms Urbanek: Patient confidentiality is an issue for us. My understanding is that Velos eResearch is very secure.

Velos: What's been your experience with Velos eResearch from a user interface perspective?

Ms Urbanek: Since we haven't launched our first study, my experience has been in setting up a protocol, and training to use Velos eResearch. Based on this experience, Velos eResearch is really straightforward to use. You don't need to be a rocket scientist to figure out how to use it.

The tools we've used in Velos eResearch thus far really fit well with what we are doing. We are particularly enthusiastic about using the patient scheduling feature in Velos when we start enrolling patients.

Velos: How would you describe life with, and without, Velos eResearch?

Ms Urbanek: I think that without Velos, we could spend a considerable amount of time re-inventing the wheel in a lot of ways.with budgeting and protocol development. Something like Velos eResearch has been needed for a long time – it fills a niche for investigators who do the same tasks over and over. I believe Velos eResearch should be very useful to a lot of investigators, since information managed in Velos can be re-used over time.

Velos: What's been your experience with Velos Support?

Ms Urbanek: Velos has been great at training our group and helping us set up our first study. It's been an enjoyable and collaborative feeling working with Velos.

Velos: Anything we can do to make things any easier?

Ms Urbanek: Nothing that I can recall. Your team does a great job listening to input and responding to that. This really makes us feel that what is important to the investigator is what you are out to achieve. I can't think of anything more you could do.

Velos: Great! Any other comments or anything you think people should know?

Ms Urbanek: As I said earlier, for organisations like us, who will be managing several, concurrent, multi-site studies, Velos eResearch can be a very useful tool. For example, in terms of protocol development, we have been developing multiple protocols with our network of clinical researchers. We have been sending these documents around by email and it has been tough to keep track of.

Velos should be very useful for us given the structure of our Network, both in the development phase, and once studies are up and running. Since it is Internet-based we should be able to support our research nurses, assist our investigators, and enable study managers to keep track of all the studies across multiple institutions.

Also for sponsors and other organisations with oversight responsibilities Velos eResearch can be a great way for them and our development team to review what is going on in the Network. And, being truly Internet-based should make all this, and my job, a whole lot easier.

Velos: Thank you, Karen.

To summarise the key points of this interview:

- Using the Internet to standardise pharma data simplifies documentation, facilitates the spread of important information and makes complex, technical projects more efficient to manage.
- These new systems applications are often not difficult to use. The main problems about conversion of processes to these systems are often more to do with the difficulty of changing old data processing habits, rather than any inherent weakness.
- Whilst some may be concerned about confidentiality arrangements associated with the Internet these can be effectively addressed and met.

In conclusion, in the future we feel confident that there will be even much greater use of innovative and effective IT approaches to cut time and increase flexibility and speed of knowledge transfer for clinical research projects.

Project Learning

Throughout the project a great deal of learning can be gained – both for the project manager and for the team generally. This learning can take many forms, including learning about:

- the feasibility of achieving the project goals (the 'what');

- the project process (the 'how');

- the capability and effectiveness of the project team;

- the organisation itself;

- the environment external to the project.

Paradoxically, the more vulnerable the project is to failure the worse a team's ability to learn is inclined to become, as they become clogged-up in a defensive mind-set. There are few teams of managers who can run counter to this tendency. Unfortunately, the brighter the managers, the more prone they tend to become to closing down the learning. Very bright people can be perfectionists and may well become allergic to recognising errors in judgements in pharma projects.

One way to counter this is to establish a balanced team (see Chapter 7, 'Influencing People and Behaviour') with a relatively detached person who acts as a type of 'chairperson' and can be more objective and dispassionate about the project.

Project Dynamics

Finally, turning to project dynamics, there are very many ways in which a project can be tracked over time. For example, to what extent does it have a deliberate, an emergent, a submergent, emergency or detergent project strategy? Also (as we see in Chapter 7), what is its difficulty over time? Fleshing out the AID analysis picture we can also ask 'What is the likely value over time of the project?'

We have already touched upon the other curves for projects, particularly the energy over time curve of the project team (Figure 6.1), and the commitment over time curve (Figure 6.2). Other curves (over time) which can be useful are:

- belief over time curves (that the project will be a success);

- confusion over time curves;

- frustration over time curves.

Ideally, the pharma project manager will tell scenario stories (in his/her head) about the future evolution of the project, and also use these visual curves to monitor where the project currently is against these scenarios.

When the project teams presented their findings a vigorous debate began about whether these problems did or did not exist. This surfacing of contentious issues is very healthy, but the project team members may feel that problems were being underplayed by members of top management.

Conclusion

Pharma projects are ones which often shift in their attractiveness, difficulty, uncertainty and in the degree of support for them over time. The amount of energy in the project team will also change. This means that project milestones are rarely givens, and that in addition to these milestones the pharma project manager may also need to track some softer indicators, too (like team energy and morale).

Systems software also offers opportunities to greatly improve the effectiveness of the drug development process.

7

Influencing People and Behaviour

Introduction

We have already seen a number of analytical techniques that will help us with pharma projects – especially in terms of managing (and influencing) people and behaviour, which involves:

- diagnosing the system of behaviour impacting on a project;

- diagnosing team roles in pharma projects;

- specific techniques for managing behaviour in projects.

The techniques we have examined in our earlier chapters include:

- 'fishbone' or root cause analysis;

- how-how analysis;

- from-to analysis;

- force-field analysis;

- stakeholder analysis;

- AID;

- assumption analysis/uncertainty;

- urgency–importance analysis.

Whilst often associated with managing the more tangible aspects of pharma projects, these techniques can be used as effectively for the softer aspects of influencing people and behaviour. For example, fishbone analysis can be used for diagnosing behavioural difficulties or constraints. How-how analysis can be used to identify strategies for influencing key stakeholders. From-to analysis helps us to establish which staff have gone through a tangible culture shift. Force-field analysis also helps us to look at the purely behavioural aspects of influencing stakeholders.

AID helps us to prioritise *which* stakeholders it is best to try to influence. The uncertainty grid assists in surfacing assumptions about the intentions and agendas of stakeholders. Finally, urgency-importance analysis provides us with a focus for prioritising our influencing efforts over time. It can also help you to prioritise which stakeholders need to be influenced – and in what order.

Nevertheless, the above techniques deal primarily with the more *analytical* aspects of managing pharma projects. Our research into the behaviour associated with projects has led us to the conclusion that equally important are the *behavioural* aspects of project management (Grundy, 1998b). Practising managers will easily recognise that the conduct of strategy itself is a battleground, given the considerable turbulence which surrounds both external and internal strategic moves. Projects, however well intentioned, become easily buffeted by strategies which are highly emergent and unpredictable. The more difficult influences are frequently behavioural in nature.

EXERCISE – PROJECTS AND BEHAVIOUR

For one project you have been involved with in the past, ask yourself:

- What were the key behaviours both within the project team and around the rest of the organisation which either:
  - facilitated the project's implementation?
  - constrained the project's implementation?
- For one or more significant constraining force:
  - why did this exist (use fishbone analysis)?
  - what could be done to ameliorate its effects?

From our earlier research (Grundy, 1998b) the strategic behaviour of an R&D team whose remit was to understand the implications (market and technological) of major changes in the external and internal environment was explored. This key department was charged with defining pharma projects which would then form a central plank of the companies' further technology. As these projects had a multi-business impact they were frequently fraught with complexity – not merely at a territorial level but also organisationally. (We will return to this research when we look at more specific techniques for understanding behaviour in projects.)

Exploring Project Behaviour

We have already seen how important stakeholders are in managing pharma projects. Stakeholders play a decisive role in determining whether projects live or die, or are condemned to that limbo of neither moving forwards nor backwards.

Indeed it is often the interaction of key individuals and larger groups which dictates the trajectory of the project. But most courses and books on project management tend to focus on creating an effective team whilst neglecting some of the more subtle and indeed complex patterns of people interaction.

We now take a look at the key variables which underpin the interactions of teams as the project develops. These variables were uncovered principally during research on senior teams working on strategy development projects in an R&D environment.

Suspecting that there were some important and new insights to be gleaned by studying project behaviour in real time, one of us was able to be a 'fly-on-the-wall' when observing a department involved in R&D strategy as described below.

The department contained a number of project teams and the management team, which met to evaluate and prioritise major projects having a major impact on its R&D strategy. The research involved a number of interviews with its managers both before and after various workshops. It also entailed observation of some of those workshops, and indeed at some point the researcher actually facilitated one (the fly being very definitely 'off-the-wall').

All of the interactions of the workshops (and the interviews) were tape-recorded and subjected to microscopic analysis and interpretation. The results were fed back to the managers, generating further illuminating data. The central output of the research is shown in Figure 7.1 which explores the behaviour associated with pharma projects.

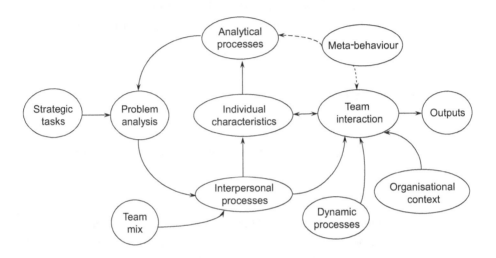

Figure 7.1   The system of pharmaceutical project behaviour

Figure 7.1 looks at this behaviour as a system. This is based on the premise that, unless all of the parts of this system are aligned well, one is likely to see dysfunctional behaviour. For instance, if the strategic tasks of the project are not appropriately defined, then the project is unlikely to exhibit harmonious behaviours. Managers will be prone to argument and frustration, spreading their energies and efforts too thinly and in sometimes opposing directions.

Equally, if the team lack analytical processes and techniques (of the kind described in this book) then they are likely to struggle in moving problems forward. But even if analytical processes are well aligned, unless managers' interpersonal processes are running smoothly again, there is likely to be significant, if not severe, disruption to behaviour.

Team mix, too, will (if it is unbalanced, or not fitting to the task) hamper project success. Many teams are assembled based either on who is available, or on the basis primarily of technical skills. It is therefore largely by accident that the team will be able to get on with each other well enough to achieve project goals. To help diagnose consistency of team roles it is a very good idea to get project members to reflect on their preferred team styles, for example using the Belbin typology. (Belbin differentiates between team styles like plant (ideas person), shaper, resource investigator, team-worker, chairman and finisher; see 'Diagnosing Team Roles' below.)

Organisational context is another key driver of behavioural harmony. An organisation where certain key team members are nervous for their jobs, or are anxious about pending promotion, will provide a rocky environment for an effective team. Also, if the organisation is extremely complex, political or divided up into disparate and opposing sets, cultures will find it hard to host effective projects.

Besides these key variables, we should also pay attention to the key outputs of the project. Where these are poorly targeted, again we are likely to see more disruptive behaviours emerging. Without clear strategic goals then personal agendas will tend to distort interactions, producing knock-on effects. Other stakeholders then dig-in or begin to play clandestine games to achieve their goals.

EXERCISE – EXPLORING PROJECT BEHAVIOUR

For two projects you have been involved with in the past, one of which went well and one of which did not go well, ask yourself:

- For the project which went well, how was alignment created behaviourally? (Use Figure 7.1 as a diagnostic technique.)
- For the project which did not go well, how was misalignment created and how were the effects then amplified in the system of strategic behaviour?

Diagnosing Team Roles

In this section we examine the mechanics of team roles. We have chosen the Belbin team-roles typology because this is not only well known, but also easy to use and robust.

Belbin team roles can be used by a team:

- to help the individual identify his/her professed team styles, and thus to help develop their personal effectiveness;

- to encourage specific individuals to try out and develop their skills in other team-role styles;

- to diagnose overall strengths and weaknesses of the entire team;

- to help manage team dynamics more effectively;

- to help plan future moves into or out of the team, and also for team formation.

Invariably, the use of Belbin team roles sparks a shift in self-awareness (and thus in effectiveness) within the team.

The key Belbin team roles are as follows:

- plant;

- shaper;

- implementer ('the company worker');

- coordinator ('chairman');

- monitor–evaluator;

- completer–finisher;

- team worker;

- resource investigator.

We now briefly describe these various roles.

PLANT

Plants are innovators and can be highly creative, providing ideas for major developments. They may prefer to work by themselves at some distance from the team, using their imagination and often working in an innovative way. They may tend to be introverted and are inclined to react to criticism and praise. Their ideas may often be 'off-the-wall' and need shaping.

The 'plant' was so named when it was found that one of the best ways to improve the performance of an ineffective and uninspired team was to 'plant' one of this team type in it. But you can also think of the plant as the team member who provides the basic ideas for growth.

The main use of a plant is to generate proposals and to solve complex problems. Plants are often needed in the initial stages of a project or when a project is failing to progress. Plants have usually made their mark as founders of companies or as originators of new products.

The tendency with plants is that they will devote too much of their creative energy to ideas which may appeal to them but do not contribute to the team's strategic and personal objectives. Plants may be put off if their ideas are rejected and may withdraw from the team, at least temporarily. It can take quite a lot of careful handling and judicious flattery (usually by the coordinator) to get the best out of a plant, but for all their faults, it is the plants who provide the vital spark.

Too many plants in one team, however, may be counter-productive as they tend to spend their time reinforcing their own ideas and engaging each other in combat.

SHAPER

Shapers are highly motivated with lots of energy. Usually they are extroverts and possess strong drive. Shapers encourage others to do things. In the face of barriers they will find a way round. Shapers are excellent at putting energy into a team and are useful in groups where politics would otherwise dominate. They are well suited to making necessary changes and do not mind taking less popular viewpoints. They will always try to impose some shape on the group discussion.

In summary, shapers see the team as an extension of their own ego. They want action and they want it immediately. There is a danger that people inside the team are likely to be steamrollered by the shaper.

IMPLEMENTER (OR 'COMPANY WORKER')

Implementers have a lot of common sense and self-control. They love hard work and like to tackle problems systematically. They are usually less concerned with the pursuit of self-interest. Implementers may lack spontaneity and not easily be able to change direction.

They are useful to an organisation because of their capacity for work and for their consistency. They succeed because they are efficient and because they have a sense of what is directly relevant and practicable. An implementer will do what needs to be done.

COORDINATOR (OR 'CHAIRPERSON')

Coordinators are able to help others to work towards shared goals. Mature and confident, they are very good at delegating and channelling activities in the pursuit of group objectives.

Co-ordinators are particularly useful when running a team with diverse skills and personal characteristics. Coordinators may well conflict with shapers due to their contrasting styles.

Coordinators see most clearly which member of the team is strong or weak in each area of the team's function and focus people on what they do best. They are conscious of the need to use the team's combined resources as effectively as possible. Coordinators define roles and work boundaries and will identify any gaps and fill them.

MONITOR–EVALUATOR

Monitor–evaluators are very sensible team members who do not get carried away by impractical ideas. They are slow decision-makers and prefer to think things over. Monitor evaluators have well-developed judgement skills but with a highly critical thinking ability.

Although monitor–evaluators are by nature critics rather than creators, they do not usually criticise just for the sake of it, but only if they can see a flaw in the project. They are often the least highly motivated of the team; enthusiasm and euphoria simply are not part of their agenda. This is compensated by their detachment and objectivity. They are also excellent in assimilating and interpreting and evaluating large volumes of complex data, and analysing problems and assessing the judgements and contributions of others.

COMPLETER–FINISHER

Completer–finishers have a huge capacity for follow-through and attention to detail. They will not start anything that they cannot finish. They tend to be anxious inside yet externally they may appear relaxed. They are typically introverted and are often not keen on delegating.

Completer–finishers are invaluable where the project requires close concentration to detail. They bring a sense of urgency to the team and are good at meeting deadlines. The completer–finisher tends not to be an assertive member of the team but generates a continuing sense of low-key urgency which keeps the team moving forward to its goals.

TEAM WORKER

Team workers help to support the team's morale. They are particularly concerned about other members of the team; they are adaptable to different situations and people, and are always diplomatic. They tend to be popular members of a group.

Team workers help to prevent interpersonal disruption within the group and thus allow all team members to contribute effectively. They will go to great lengths to avoid interpersonal clashes. As a promoter of team harmony, the team worker counterbalances the tensions which can be caused by the shaper and the plant.

RESOURCE INVESTIGATOR

Resource investigators are often enthusiastic extroverts. They are good at networking with people both inside and outside the team. They are adept at exploring new opportunities and developing contacts. They are particularly good at picking up other people's ideas and developing them. They are also skilled at finding out what is available and what can be done, and about finding useful data for the pharma project, perhaps from the Internet.

EXERCISE – WHICH BELBIN TEAM ROLE CORRESPONDS TO YOUR OWN?

Based on your reading of the previous team-role typologies, score yourself as follows:

	Hardly applies at all	Applies a little	Applicable	Very applicable	Extremely applicable
	1	2	3	4	5
Plant					
Shaper					
Implementer					
Coordinator					
Monitor–evaluator					
Completer–finisher					
Team worker					
Resource investigator					

What is the 'so-what?' from this analysis, particularly:

- Which are your two most favoured role styles and what significance does this have?
- What are your two least favoured role styles and what significance does this have?
- What effect does this have on how you operate in your current team?

In the pharma industry there is often a lack of plants, shapers, and coordinator (chairperson), and this can be a cause of project disappointments, and perhaps failure.

Following on from this analysis it is useful to examine how Belbin team roles impact on the strategic thinking and implementation work which complex pharma projects imply.

- Plant: generates off-the-wall ideas which feed into breakthrough thinking. But on its own these ideas may be half-formed, underdeveloped and may fail in practice.

- Shaper: helps to develop ideas into workable strategies.

- Implementer: actually helps get the implementation done.

- Coordinator: brings together the ideas of different team members and reconciles them. Also establishes the key roles so people know what they are doing.

- Monitor–evaluator: helps to make the ideas into an effective business case – and monitors results.

- Completer–finisher: maintains a focus on project milestones.

- Team worker: harmonises team interaction and its personal agendas.

- Resource investigator: ensures that interfaces with the organisational environment happen smoothly.

Specific Techniques for Understanding Behaviour

In this section we divide one of the key techniques for understanding the behaviour associated with major pharma projects into two categories: agenda analysis and dynamic analysis. In each case we critique the potential problems and difficulties which might arise when implementing them – together with their possible solution.

These techniques include:

Agenda analysis

- personal and strategic agenda (PASTA factor analysis) – and understanding sub-personalities.

Dynamic analysis

- behavioural scenarios;

- difficulty over time, energy over time, and frustration over time curves.

BEHAVIOURAL SCENARIOS

Behavioural scenarios involve semi-structured story-telling about how the future of the pharma project may develop. A first technique is to plot some key assumptions concerning the behavioural influences in the project. Figure 7.2 illustrates these, also identifying where certain behavioural assumptions which might have seemed to have been either of less importance or lesser uncertainty can quickly move into the south-east of the uncertainty grid – its 'danger zone'.

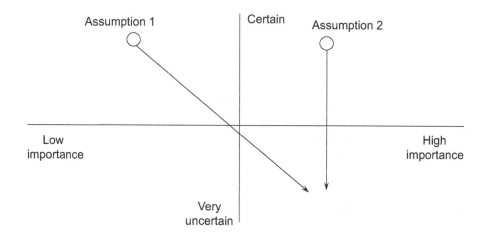

Figure 7.2   A behavioural uncertainty–importance grid

Where one or more assumptions occur in this danger zone, it is at that point that a particular behavioural scenario can be drawn out. One scenario thus may be that the project team leader resigns and is then replaced by another team leader – who then immediately conducts an entire review of the pharma project with the result being a radical change in its direction.

Behavioural scenarios (as above) can be refined by story-telling. For example, one can pick out 'transitional behavioural events'. These events will lead us from the current state of the pharma project to one which is quite different. Or, one might start off with a particular future and then work backwards to define the kind of behavioural story-line which might lead up to that scenario (as in the 1985 science fiction comedy film *Back to the Future*).

A potential problem with using behavioural scenarios is that it is very possible that the scenario turns out to be completely wrong (for example, where a new drug fails in clinical trials or to meet ethical committee approval). The very nature of scenarios makes the possibility of mis-judging the future a significant risk. However the alternatives – either of not looking into the behavioural future or extrapolating from the behavioural past – do not seem viable. If there is real doubt that one particular scenario fails to tease-out the main behavioural turning points, then you might consider developing a second or even a third one.

Or, one might use the metaphor model of the uncertainty tunnel which we saw earlier in the book to help understand:

• the behavioural antecedents of the projects;

• the factors which might amplify or dampen behavioural change affecting the project;

• the first, second or third order behavioural consequence of any important and sensitive event within or outside the pharma project.

EXERCISE – BEHAVIOURAL SCENARIOS

For one key pharma project which you are currently involved in, ask yourself:

• What behavioural interactions might you foresee as impacting on the project medium-term (positive or negative)?
• What specific stories can you tell about how the various actors within the project team might deal with each other?
• In what a scenario (if any) do all behaviours become aligned?
• What could you now do to help bring about this (positive) behavioural wishbone?

Let us now look at how we can use analytical techniques to diagnose some of the behavioural issues around pharma projects.

A cause-of-behaviour analysis (COBRA) helps us to do this and is shown in Figure 7.3.

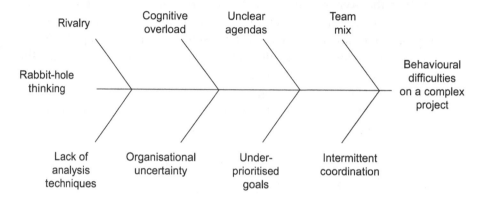

Figure 7.3   Cause-of-behaviour analysis

In project meetings there is often a tendency for key members of the pharma project team to focus on more microscopic issues (involving them often going off at a tangent), rather than holding their attention at a more 'helicopter level'. Subsequent feedback showing the level and dynamics of discussion (see Figure 7.4) helped one project team to understand the dysfunctional effects of excessive 'picking apart' behaviour. Figure 7.4 now shows a typical discussion going through high, medium or low levels of generality. This technique did prove helpful in discerning *who* in the team had the greatest tendency to 'rabbit hole' the discussions, and is a useful mental aid for any pharma project facilitator.

When project teams gain a narrower focus of attention they are frequently more able to share the cognitive maps and assumptions of its key individuals, producing far greater momentum and harmony in its behaviours. So the greater the *cognitive clarity* exists within a project team, other things being equal, the less behavioural turbulence is likely to exist.

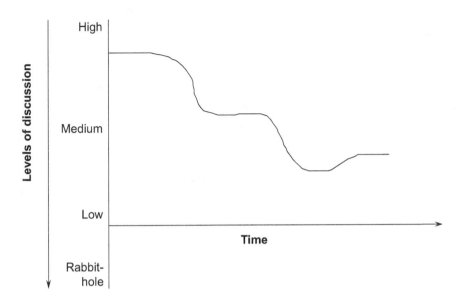

Figure 7.4   Levels of discussion

Certain behavioural drivers often have the tendency to govern the cognitive subject matter of managers. The main drivers of this are the *personal agendas* of individuals. These agendas contained a mix of emotion, territorial and cognitive elements which are all highly intermingled.

In other words, when managers argue about a particular project, whilst they may seem to be debating its real business parameters, they are often very much under the influence of their personal agendas. These can include attachment to doing the project a certain way, fear of failure and personal identification with the project. These personal agendas need to be distinguished from the business agendas. Stakeholder analysis (see Chapter 4) is especially helpful here. Sometimes the personal identification with the project can become so strong that one or more individuals may even control the team members' ability to have ideas about the project's very significance – and how it should be done. We call this the project's 'ideas territory'. This is very common in drug development projects.

This notion of 'ideas territory' is likely to be very helpful elsewhere, especially when a particular pharma project is complex and where a particular idea of 'how it will work or not work' can come to dominate the wider project team's thinking. And to challenge the dominant ideas territory is to make as much of a *political* challenge as it is to challenge the specific influence and power of an individual.

Finally, to improve international understanding in the influencing process, we need good cross-cultural communication:

- at head office – affiliate liaison;

- at the beginning of international study planning;

- in training;

- in auditing.

Some key tips for improving cross-cultural communication are:

- Be aware of local customs and expectations, for example:

    - northern Europeans leave pauses in speech, southern Europeans tend not to;
    - Japanese doctors do not explain treatment, therefore, explaining informed consent is difficult.

- Be aware of national symbols, heroes and rituals.

- For native English speakers:

    - KISS – Keep it Short and Simple.

- Speak slowly, use pauses and explain.

- Be aware of vocabulary and its connotations.

- Use signposting, for example:

    - saying 'now let's turn to.', 'lets move on...'

- Check the listener's understanding:

    - 'am I right in thinking...'

- Use simple words, simple sentence construction.

- Read e-mails to check meaning.

- Spell-check emails to minimise confusion.

- Beware use of idioms and metaphors – what is understood? For example, 'grasping the bull by the horns...'

- Be careful making jokes – cross-cultural communication can make work.

Conclusion

Influencing people and behaviour is a fundamental part of contemporary pharma project management. This 'softer' area of project management requires a combination of analytical skill, vision, leadership and imagination and also proactive management of team roles.

The analytical tools – like fishbone (cause-of-behaviour analysis) and stakeholder analysis will be indispensable to you in managing these softer aspects of pharma projects.

It also requires interpersonal sensitivity coupled with the necessary political determination to translate your vision for the pharma project into a reality.

8

Project Management Checklists and Cost-management Project Case Study

Introduction

In this practical chapter we give you some detailed checklists for managing pharma projects, beginning first with a very specific and detailed example of over 100 activities for an effective multi-centre clinical trial. This is followed by more general areas such as:

- organic development projects, generally (including drug development);

- organisational change projects (including a stage-by-stage process and application-specific checklists);

- acquisition and alliance (joint venture) projects (increasingly important in the pharma industry).

You should use these checklists when tackling any particular type of pharma project. They can be used for:

- developing your own project plans;

- appraising the project plans of others.

We also look at a case study on project managing cost breakthroughs in the pharma industry.

Checklist for Multicentre Clinical Research Trials

The following detailed checklist takes you through each chronological stage of planning a clinical research multicentre trial. Running multicentre clinical trials is complex, with a large number of activities to undertake. Since clinical research projects typically have a number of activities which are usually the same in clinical trials.

The list of activities has been found by participants of clinical research project management courses ran by the authors to be very helpful in planning such trials. The list illustrates how thoroughly you need to project manage a clinical trial, one of the most frequent and important applications of project management within the pharma industry.

Four to six months before the study starts to recruit patients:

1. Obtain a brief from the Project Sponsor which defines the clinical trial objectives, rationale, outline timeframe, and estimated budget available.   ☐

2. Review literature and other available information.   ☐

3. Discuss the therapeutic areas with experts in the company and externally such as key opinion leaders, patient groups may also be of help.   ☐

4. Decide on the study design potential locations for the study (for example, which countries have a high incidence of the disease, where do you propose to market the drug.   ☐

5. Identify potential locations for the study (for example, which countries have a high incidence of the disease, where do you propose to market the drug.   ☐

6. Obtain statistical input to calculate sample sizes and prepare the statistical plan.   ☐

7. Ensure availability of suitable non-clinical and clinical research data (for example, phase I, phase II) information to justify carrying out this clinical study.   ☐

8.   Prepare an outline of the protocol.   ☐

9.   If the study is carried out in the EU obtain the European Clinical Trials Database (EUDRACT) number in accordance with the Clinical Trial Directive requirements.   ☐

10.   Start to prepare the outline plan for the study using the WBS technique, outline Gantt chart with estimated timelines for main activities of the study.   ☐

11.   Identify possible project risks and uncertainties. Prepare a risk register to handle risks – develop contingencies and ways to mitigate risks.   ☐

12.   Identify which departments are going to be involved in the study and start to identify key people from these departments who will be a part of the study team.   ☐

13.   Prepare the a list of key stakeholders for the project.   ☐

14.   Decide on test drug(s) and comparator drug(s).   ☐

15.   Check availability of study medication and place provisional order so as to prevent this becoming a rate limiting activity. The exact quantities can be refined later. Ensure the qualified person (QP) has been contacted in order to help prevent delays in obtaining the study medication.   ☐

16.   Prepare a contingency plan for unavailability of comparator drugs in some countries.   ☐

17.   Decide on detailed timelines for study preparation, performance and evaluation, including critical time points.   ☐

18.   Start some initial feasibility studies into the countries of interest. ☐

19.   Ensure investigator brochure is available and if new (this is if new information is available or the brochure has not been updated in the last year).   ☐

20. Identify and decide on study management technologies and processes, that is, specific project management software to be used in the study, is the study going to use EDC.   ☐

Four months before

1. Consider outline resources needed and whether to use a CRO or freelance consultants for the study.   ☐

2. Decide on countries involved, number of sites, and number of subjects per site.   ☐

3. Identify investigators – databases, recommendations, conferences, directories and so on.   ☐

4. Design a feasibility study plan including assessing potential investigators ability to recruit patients.   ☐

5. Perform the feasibility study.   ☐

6. Start to carry out study site assessment visits.   ☐

7. Decide on criteria for deciding final list of potential investigators.   ☐

8. Prepare subject recruitment strategy plan for the study including assessing options for recruitment – including advertising.   ☐

9. Prepare a contingency plan for patient recruitment problems.   ☐

10. Start preparation of the investigator brochure if not already available.   ☐

11. Check order for study medication to see if it is progressing on time.   ☐

12. Prepare a contingency plan for delayed availability of study medication.   ☐

13. Identify labelling and importation requirements for the study medication to meet the requirements of different countries involved in the study.   ☐

14. Decide on the packaging and shipment strategy.   ☐

15. Prepare a contingency plan for packaging and shipping delays. ☐

16. Plan a detailed project team structure.   ☐

17. Identify project team members and their roles and responsibilities. ☐

18. Prepare a written brief of the roles and responsibilities of the team members.

19. Prepare a detailed resource plan for the overall study in terms of people and equipment.   ☐

20. Decide on a resource contingency plan.   ☐

21. Implement study management technologies and train project team.   ☐

22. Find vendors for outsourced study activities and technologies or use preferred vendors already being used for other studies. ☐

23. Prepare vendors' briefing documents so that vendors can provide proposals for you to decide who to use.   ☐

24. Assess proposals from vendors.   ☐

25. Decide on a short list of vendors.   ☐

26. Audit short-listed vendors.   ☐

27. Decide which vendors to use.   ☐

28. Prepare and sign contracts for vendors.   ☐

Three months before:

1. Prepare, organise, review and finalise communication plan with project team, vendors, and investigators. ☐

2. Order study medication packaging. ☐

3. Decide on subject recruitment activities. ☐

4. Prepare key study draft key study documents, for example, protocol, CRF, drug accountability documentation, monitors' manual. ☐

5. Decide on the strategy for investigators' meeting(s). ☐

6. Plan an investigator meeting, negotiate budget (consider using a commercial organisation to organiser the investigator meeting(s) or delegate to a member of the study team – this is a mini-project on its own). ☐

7. Decide on venue(s) and date(s) and prepare investigators' meeting(s). ☐

8. Prepare a template for investigator contracts. ☐

9. Plan and organise study pre-study site visits. ☐

10. Negotiate terms and conditions of contract with investigators and other people at the site, for example, the pharmacy. ☐

11. Decide on final list of investigators. ☐

12. Finalise the detailed study budget and obtain approval from project sponsor. ☐

13. Prepare a contingency plan for delays in budget negotiations and approval. ☐

14. Prepare a study regulatory approval and ethics committee submission plan – what is required in each country and for each site. ☐

15. Prepare a contingency plan for ethics committee and study approval delays and/or problems.   ☐

16. Review draft protocol and plan and manage the review process. This can often be a rate limiting activity.   ☐

17. Organise the quality assurance check of protocol and ensure the CRF is available at this time.   ☐

18. Prepare final protocol.   ☐

19. Organise translation of any documents, according to local requirements.   ☐

20. Finalise contracts with investigators and/or investigator institution.   ☐

21. Prepare standard patient informed consent documentation.   ☐

22. Prepare the centre-specific informed consent/patient information sheet.   ☐

23. Define and organise translation requirements for consent document.   ☐

24. Plan and manage review process for consent process in different countries.   ☐

25. Prepare standard consent documents per country.   ☐

26. Prepare advertisement plus other subject-and/or investigator-related information material.   ☐

27. Plan and manage the review process for advertisement and additional information material in the different countries.   ☐

28. Finalise advertisement and additional information material.   ☐

29. Prepare, organise, review and finalise CRF.   ☐

30. Prepare, organise, review and finalise investigators' brochure.   ☐

31. Organise translations of study material according to local requirements. ☐

32. Plan the individual submissions to ethics committees in each country. ☐

33. Prepare, organise, review and finalise the ethics committee submission packages for all investigators. ☐

34. Prepare, organise, review and finalise study regulatory authorisation for each country in the trial. ☐

Two months before:

1. Submit to ethics committees (and regulatory authorities in countries with 'parallel submission' if Clinical Trail Directive country legislation allow this). ☐

2. Liase with the audit department for them to prepare, manage, review and finalise audit plan. ☐

3. Prepare drug labels. ☐

4. Confirm site selection and budgetary-specific needs, including resources. ☐

5. Collect all legally required information from investigators (that is, essential regulatory documents and contracts). ☐

6. Collect information on national serious adverse event (SAE) and adverse event (AE) handling requirements. ☐

7. Prepare, organise, review and finalise data management plan. ☐

8. Plan and organise printing of the CRF (including enough 'reserve' CRFs if using paper CRFs rather than electronic. ☐

9. Prepare, manage, review and finalise the CRF convention manual. ☐

10. Prepare, organise, review, and finalise the monitors' manual to help monitors answer questions about the study and ensure CRFs are completed to a high standard.   ☐

11. Prepare training material for the project team – particularly the monitors.   ☐

12. Prepare, organise, review and finalise the SAE and AE handling plan.   ☐

13. Prepare, organise, review and finalise the safety database.   ☐

14. Verify roles and responsibilities for key processes, such as safety.   ☐

15. Prepare, organise, review and finalise database.   ☐

16. Finalise statistical plan.   ☐

Four to six weeks before:

1. Prepare investigator site master files, for example, for the investigator team and pharmacy (if applicable).   ☐

2. Hold a monitors' meeting to train the monitors and other project team members.   ☐

3. Hold investigators' meeting(s).   ☐

4. Hold start-up meeting with project team and vendors.   ☐

5. Ensure study approval and drug importation licenses are in place.   ☐

6. Manage study drug and material shipment to sites.   ☐

7. Plan and set up the investigator fees payment process.   ☐

8. Plan study initiation activities.   ☐

9. Ensure all study drugs and material arrived at sites.   ☐

10.   Perform study initiation visits at sites including training the study team – coordinators and other involved at the site staff.   ☐

11.   Subject recruitment can start once the ethics approval and regulatory aspects have been processed, and any other initiation aspects are in place.   ☐

This checklist has been derived from Verney and Kingmann, 'A 6 month Process for Planning Multi-centre Clinical Trials', *Applied Clinical Trials*, February 2003, pp. 58–61.

Checklists for Organic Business Development Projects

We have already given you some processes for evaluating major pharma projects in Chapter 5. These checklists will help to flesh out some of the richer content issues which you may well come up against. While managers may feel they are well-versed in these organic development projects, they may well look too myopically at the more obvious areas of inquiry.

Organic business development projects can be aimed at a number of areas including:

• new drug development;

• new market development – by sector or by geography;

• new distribution channels;

• new technologies.

NEW DRUG DEVELOPMENT

Drug development brings together strategic issues, technical considerations, and operational and organisational implications. Our questions on new drug development are:

1.   How fast is the market for this type of drug growing?

2.   How much competitive pressure is in its market?

3.   How well is the drug likely to meet its target customer needs; in terms of likely efficacy, side-effects and ease of use?

4.   Which other drugs is it competing with and what are the relative advantages/disadvantages between each?

5.   Does the drug have any wonderfully innovative benefits (which add real value)?

6.   If these exist, how easily can these be imitated or satisfied through alternative therapeutic treatments?

7.   How consistent is the organisation's capability and mind-set with this drug, and what implementation issues might this raise?

8.   What skills training is required to support this drug effectively?

9.   Are the drug's long-run unit costs likely to be sustainable longer-term?

10.   What other changes in the organisation (for example, to key business processes or to organisational structure) are needed?

11.   Will the sales force and distribution channels accommodate the new drug effectively – without destruction, disruption or a dilution of sales of other drugs?

12.   To what extent might the product cannibalise on other existing drugs?

13.   To what extent will the drugs innovation be effectively project-managed?

14.   How can its introduction be positioned and accelerated in the organisation?

NEW MARKET DEVELOPMENT PROJECTS

New market development projects may overlap to some extent with new products. Nevertheless, we include some new questions to supplement those:

1.   Have you systematically prioritised which (of potential new markets) it would be most attractive to address (for example, using the AID analysis, or the project option grid)?

2.   How inherently attractive is this market (consider its growth drivers and the level of competitive pressure)?

3.   How difficult is it to operate within that market?

4.   Do we have the natural competencies to do well in that market?

5.   Is this market culturally vastly different to our current core markets?

6.   Is this a market especially prone to high costs of servicing our target patients or distribution channels, or low margins generally?

7.   Have we got a genuinely 'cunning' entry strategy (or just an average one)?

8.   What are the most critical uncertainties about that market and how can we minimise our exposure to these?

9.   Will entering this particular market foreclose options to enter other markets, for example due to resource constraints?

10.   To what extent will market conditions vary internationally, and which of these markets should we really give highest priority?

NEW DISTRIBUTION CHANNEL PROJECTS

Opening up new distribution channels avoids the difficulties of new drug and/or market innovation – and may well be relatively cheap. But in order to avoid diluting our strategy and shareholder value, we will need to be relatively selective, as follows:

1.   How much margin are we likely to obtain from a new distribution channel?

2.   How difficult is it likely to be to deal with?

3.   What are the key alternatives to dealing with this particular channel (for example, by the Internet, sales force, an alliance, and so on)?

4.   Will this particular channel lead to conflict with any other distribution channels and, if so, how will we manage it?

5.   Are we likely to get a high level of returns or other quality problems through this channel?

6.   Will the channel actually understand our product portfolio sufficiently well?

7.   How much support will this channel put behind our product – relative to that of other products?

8.   Does this distribution channel have something that fits our natural competencies and our culture?

9.   How competitive is this particular channel relative to other pathways to market?

10.   If we do not use this channel, what (if anything) is the biggest downside?

11.   How would we project manage new entry to that channel?

NEW TECHNOLOGIES

New technologies might include new ways of applying a drug therapy to patients. These new technologies may be a turn-on to middle managers but might be a turn-off to some top managers (whose main focus is frequently to extract short- and medium-term value out of the business). We may therefore need some testing questions in order to screen innovative technology projects:

1.   Does the technology actually fit with our present or emerging definition of 'what business(es) we are in'?

2.   Do we really understand the technology?

3.   What other things (other than technology) all have to line up to deliver real value? (Use a 'wishbone' analysis.)

4. Are we doing the project mainly because of its sheer technological edge, and because it is inherently exciting – or because it will generate real value, and value that we can actually harvest?

5. What key value and cost drivers are impacted on by the new technology?

6. What new skills do we need to fully exploit any new technology?

7. To what extent do we have to change our mind-set in order to get the very best out of the new technology?

8. Where the technology relies heavily on the Internet, how easy is our business model copied or imitated?

9. How quickly will the new technology spread and where there are customer turn-offs in its use, how can these be mitigated or removed?

10. How rapidly might the technology be superseded by further technologies and how vulnerable does this therefore make our strategy?

11. What substitute technologies are available which are in many respects better right now?

12. How should we project manage the introduction of the new technology?

Checklists for Organisational Change Projects

The checklists in this section are designed to provide managers with a lasting guide to helping them manage change on a day-to-day basis within the pharma industry. This applies at the organisational level, at the level of more specific areas of change and also with managers' individual roles. The checklists are structured in three parts as follows:

1. project managing the change process, including project definition, strategy, planning, implementation, control, learning;

2.   analysing content issues, externally, internally and cross-functionally;

3.   managing specific change applications, including for example, restructuring, quality, and culture change.

PROJECT MANAGING THE CHANGE PROCESS

The key phases of project managing change within the pharma industry are:

1.   project definition;

2.   strategy and planning;

3.   implementation;

4.   control and learning.

Typically most change projects in the pharma industry focus principally upon their implementation with the other phases being given less attention to diagnosis and also to the change strategy.

Project definition

1.   Have we identified the real nature of the 'change problem' or 'opportunity'?

2.   Have we diagnosed 'where we currently are'?

3.   Is the objective of the change clearly specified in terms of where we want to be and with what tangible benefits and by when?

4.   How wide is the gap between where we are now and where we need to be, and how does this stack up against preconceived ideas of how long and difficult the change process will be?

5.   What are the key enabling and constraining forces (that is, a force-field analysis) within both the change and its context which will influence progress towards meeting the change objectives?

6.   Have these 'key change forces' picked up both tangible and less tangible factors as they now are (that is, not in terms of an 'ideal') in the change process, for example:

- leadership;
- communication;
- skills;
- key stakeholders;
- readiness for change;
- culture and style;
- systems;
- adequacy of resources;
- timescales;
- clarity of change plans.

7.   Do any of these forces identify possible 'stoppers'?

8.   What is the overall 'balance' of forces – do these show the change as being 'manageable', 'very difficult' or as 'mission impossible?

9.   Has the strategy for the pharma change now been reshaped in the light of the force-field analysis?

10. Has a stakeholder analysis been performed in order to ensure (a) the force-field analysis is complete, and (b) to evolve influencing strategies to help mobilise commitment to change?

Strategy and planning

A particularly important activity is developing an effective strategy for the pharma change project before detailed change plans are laid down:

1.   Has the overall change objective (per the definition phase) been refined into a small number of more detailed and specific change objectives?

2.   What are the key strategic options for how the pharma change project will be implemented and how are these positioned on the AID grid?

3.   Are these objectives supported by key change milestones which specify:

  • phases of the change process?
  • clear outputs and outcomes of each phase?
  • who is responsible for achieving these milestones?

4.   Has a network of appropriately resourced activities been drawn up to support the achievement of these milestones?

5.   Has the change project been thoroughly evaluated in terms of tangible and less tangible benefits and costs and who are these 'owned' by in the organisation?

6.   What key risks and uncertainties have been identified? Does this include interdependencies with other areas of change and possible changes in management intent?

7.   Have the initial force-field analysis and stakeholder analysis been updated for further changes since the diagnosis phase?

8.   Has an appropriate and competent leader of the change been appointed and does he or she have a change project team with adequate skills and an appropriate style to ensure smooth implementation?

9.   Has the change project been suitably communicated in a skilfully targeted and timed way to *all* those playing a central role in the change *and* those indirectly affected by the change?

10. Do business plans adequately reflect any unavoidable drop in performance due to the inherent problems of managing a particularly difficult transition?

11. Is there an explicit business case for any major change?

Implementation

The implementation of any pharma change project can be very frustrating as the project fails to mobilise or suffers multiple setbacks. This calls for a number of questions, as follows:

1.   Where key milestones are not being met does this suggest that:

- the 'problem' has not been properly defined in the first place?
- the constraints are more severe than expected or new and unforeseen constraints surface?
- the communication strategy did not work?
- there is a problem of leadership or skills, or both?
- the capability to digest change is less than was previously thought?
- the change process requires more resource than first thought, or has been delayed or starved of resource?
- new (antagonistic) stakeholders have emerged or support from once favourable stakeholders has ebbed away?

2.   If the symptoms of (1) above were being experienced, then does this suggest that the overall pharma change strategy needs to be revisited?

3.   How can action plans now be tailored to accelerate progress or remove bottlenecks?

4.   What new contingencies and risks have emerged and how might action plans be strengthened to deal with these?

CONTROL AND LEARNING

Besides difficulties in implementation we may also need to address the extent to which the pharma change project has been effectively controlled and also what learning has come out of it?

1.   Are the milestones of the pharma change project being met in terms of:

- tangible benefits?
- less tangible benefits?
- tangible costs?
- less tangible costs?
- timings?

2.   How effectively has the change process been implemented relative to:

- past experience within the business area?
- past experience of business areas elsewhere in the organisation?
- other organisations undertaking similar change?

3.   Have change management processes been applied consistently throughout the change project, including:

- monitoring of enablers for and constraints to change and regular stakeholder analysis?
- project management systems for planning, control and feedback?

4.   Did the pharma change project actually meet its key objectives and, if not, why not?

5.   What should we now do, therefore, to secure the intended benefits of the change?

6.   How might we influence key stakeholders to commit to any further necessary or appropriate change?

7.   What lessons can now be drawn about:

- how we diagnose, plan, implement and control change generally?
- our overall capacity for and capability to implement change?

8.   How can we disseminate these 'learning lessons' in an open way, and without embarrassment?

ANALYSIS OF CONTENT ISSUES

Besides the above process issues we may need to do a healthcheck on some of the more content issues of the project, including:

1.   Does the change project involve several departments across the pharma company and if so how does this impact on how change is managed?

2.   To what extent does it involve external parties and stakeholders including customers, suppliers, regulatory authorities, and so on – have they been brought on board with the change?

3.   Is the change project seen as a 'quick fix' (less than six months), a 'medium-term campaign' (between six and 18 months) or a 'long campaign' (between 18 months and five years) and is this timescale realistic?

4.   Is this change resource-intensive in terms of internal technical skills, external skills or management time and will this be forthcoming?

5.   What is the critically perceived degree of difficulty of the change management:

   • technically?
   • politically?

and is this fully reflected in the change strategy?

6.   Does the change involve cross-border management and linguistic and cultural differences and, if so, how will these be managed?

7.   Is the change project amenable to benchmarking? If not, how is it proposed to keep an objective track of benefits yielded and on the effectiveness of the change process?

8.   Has an analysis of 'key change issues' showing key interrelationships between these issues been completed?

9.   Have *all* the relevant content issues been surfaced, for example using:

   • force-field analysis?
   • stakeholder analysis?
   • analysing the systems of change (strategy, structure, culture and style, people and skills, systems)?

10. Have the 'soft' and less tangible issues been given sufficient emphasis in analysing the change or does it feel as if managers want

to short-cut or just do not appreciate or think about the importance of these issues in the steps of change required?

SPECIFIC CHANGE APPLICATIONS

Introduction

Before we leave organisational change projects in the pharma industry certain types of projects warrant special attention as follows. A number of common applications now come up regularly as key problems facing managers. These include:

- restructuring;

- change in specific roles and style;

- quality management;

- culture change;

- information systems.

We deal with each of these projects in some depth below.

Restructuring projects

Restructuring projects are now undertaken on an almost routine basis by most pharma companies, both due to ongoing business change and due to post acquisition. Restructuring is often managed in relative isolation from other change and is also positioned as geared towards delivering more shorter-term benefits. Restructuring – if managed as a project – can be handled much more effectively than this, especially if the following questions are addressed:

1. Is the rationale for the restructuring fully thought through and does this reflect not merely current needs but anticipate pending changes in the business?

2. Is there a history of frequent re-structuring which results in a permanent (and unnecessary) state of instability in the organisation?

3.   Has the restructuring put managers into 'artificial' positions without genuine business benefits which are patently transparent and which will aggravate organisational ambiguity?

4.   Are new appointees genuinely capable of being effective in their roles given their skills, their style, and also the degree of team-working within the organisation?

5.   Has the restructuring been communicated in such a way to lay bare the business-led reasons for the restructuring?

6.   What is the timing of announcement of restructuring – has it been deliberately timed so as to prevent reflection and debate and thereby result in simmering resentment?

7.   How does the restructuring complement other projects or initiatives in the business and how should it be managed alongside these?

Change projects in specific roles and management style

1.   Has the change project been thoroughly thought through in terms of:

- tangible benefits and costs?
- less tangible benefits and costs?
- risks to the business?

2.   Have all the knock-on effects of the change project been thought through (for instance, on the bosses and subordinates of those whose roles have changed – not only in terms of the content of responsibilities but also in terms of style)?

3.   By what method have staff been chosen to be appointed or re-appointed to positions (for example, have they gone through a thorough and recent assessment of their competencies)?

Quality management projects

Quality management projects in the pharma industry are both important and need to be project managed (especially during manufacturing and in clinical studies) as follows:

How does the 'quality management' initiative link in with the organisation's underlying paradigm (especially in its controls, routines, rituals and overall culture)?

1. Is the organisation (and particularly senior management) prepared for a 'long haul' on quality?

2. Is the focus of quality management mainly internal or is it inextricably linked with competitive strategy?

3. Does this focus flow through to external benchmarking of external value delivered to customers and also to benchmarking of key internal processes?

4. Have expectations of managers been set appropriately from the outset during all communications to prevent 'early cynicism'?

5. Are top management prepared to mirror quality in their own behaviour and style?

6. Which (specific) senior managers are *least* likely to behave in ways which show an active 'enthusiasm for quality'?

7. Is 'quality management' made equally applicable to major management processes (for example, strategic planning, performance review and individual appraisals) as well as to more specific 'operational' issues?

8. Has it been generally accepted in the organisation that 'quality management' involves a major (and strategic) change or is it seen merely as a 'good initiative' to be doing?

9. Is there a balance between the measurement and control of performance (which quality management may imply) versus 'trust' and 'empowerment' at the individual and team level as part of a 'quality culture'?

10. Is the emphasis on quality in danger of becoming a new 'ritual' without regard for which aspects of quality are of greatest strategic value?

11.   Is there an appropriate balance of effort between efforts to rectify quality disadvantage versus efforts to achieve a distinctive advantage through quality?

Culture change projects

Many major pharma companies (such as GSK) in the 1990s went through culture change initiatives (often initiated after mergers) which were project managed with varying success. The need to re-orientate organisational mind-sets is unlikely to go away in the new millennium and the following questions are therefore as applicable as ever:

1.   What is the fundamental reason for launching an attempt to manage 'culture change projects'. Is it, for example:

   * to get rid of the 'bureaucracy'?
   * to reduce complexity and cost?
   * to focus on 'the customer' – internal or external?
   * to remedy competitive disadvantage?
   * to amplify the power base of a new leader?

2.   Is this linked to tangible areas of change projects such as restructuring, role redefinition, bringing in 'new blood', physical relocation to a new site, or to a change in ownership or status of the business? If not, how is it proposed to make the change happen without making changes of a tangible nature?

3.   Has the scope of the change project been fully addressed (for instance, does it cover head office, business units, international businesses – does it also penetrate a number of levels of management and operational staff)?

4.   How central is the 'culture change project' positioned in the organisation with visible and ongoing backing of top management?

5.   How will culture change effects (positive and negative) be monitored?

6.   How will management track the value of the culture change project through tangible and less tangible impact on performance?

7.   How sustainable will efforts to change the culture be – for one, three, four or more years (and at what cost)?

8.   How will 'new stories' within the 'emerging paradigm' be identified and broadcast?

9.   Will the culture change project have tangible bite – will we be prepared to remove or sideline major antagonists?

10.   How will we address the problem of 'decoy behaviour' (or behaviour paying merely lip-service to change)?

Information systems projects

Life in today's pharma organisation is almost unrecognisable with the expansion of office technology and communications, for example in document management.

The pharma industry is knowledge and data intensive, and information processing capability is a major cost driver and also a key influence on time-to-market. Information systems projects are also demanding at a business, technical, cultural and, especially, political level. Therefore consider the following:

1.   Are all your projects aimed at changing information systems part of an overall information strategy which is, in turn, linked to both business strategy and intended organisational change?

2.   How have the cost/benefits of any change project been evaluated in terms of both internal and external benefits and costs, including:

  • access to distribution channels?
  • improving responsiveness?
  • operational efficiency and capacity?

3.   Are changes in information systems seen as (a) primarily of a technical issue, versus (b) as also generating important and more difficult people-related and political issues? In the latter case, does the organisation have the necessary tools (like stakeholder analysis) and processes to gain maximum ownership for change?

4.   Who are the key stakeholders (a) of the end outputs of information systems, and (b) as agents within the change process itself?

5.   Is there a risk of overrun against required timescales which might result in an expensive and disruptive 'crash programme' or a dilution of project benefits?

Checklists for Acquisitions and Alliances (Joint Venture) Projects

Acquisitions and alliances (or joint ventures) are increasingly important within the pharma industry as companies continually compete globally – and try to reduce costs. In these checklists we first deal with acquisitions and we then we move on to alliances.

ACQUISITION PROJECTS

Acquisitions are notoriously difficult projects to manage – before, during and after the deal – both within and outside the pharma industry. They combine a multiplicity of management processes and perspectives including ones from:

- strategic management;

- financial management;

- operations management;

- organisation and people management;

- specialist disciplines like taxation and legal.

Besides complexity of content, pharma acquisitions are also equally complex in terms of process. They involve multi-disciplinary team-working, and often to tight deadlines. There is considerable uncertainty within the process, as acquisitions involve negotiation between at least two key parties – the vendor and the acquirer – and also their professional advisers (of whom there will be many).

There are also likely to be other stakeholders including group head office, besides the acquiring business unit itself.

Acquisitions need to be managed through a number of key stages, as follows:

1.   setting strategy and objectives;

2.   acquisition evaluation;

3.   negotiating the deal;

4.   integration;

5.   post-review and learning.

We deal with each of these stages below.

Setting strategy and objectives

Acquisitions of pharma businesses often lack a robust strategy. To avoid this we must ask the following:

1.   What is our own strategic position, and is it strong, average or weak?

2.   What strategic options (generally) for corporate development – alongside and including acquisition – do we have?

3.   Do we have the natural capabilities to screen and evaluate acquisitions (without getting carried away with the 'thrill of the chase') and also to negotiate a favourable deal and to integrate it effectively?

4.   Is this a good time for us to be thinking about acquisitions (for example, in terms of the financial markets generally)?

5.   More specifically, what are our most important objectives for making an acquisition and are these good or bad?

      'Good reasons' for making an acquisition might include:

      • increasing our own shareholder value so we can add tangible value to the acquired business;

- to acquire scarce capabilities (for example, management or technical skills) that we can apply elsewhere;
- building our own competitive advantage.

'Bad reasons' for making an acquisition might include:

- to grow the business (as an end in itself);
- to enhance our own, personal careers;
- because we feel threatened by increased competition;
- because others are doing it, and we might get left behind.

6.   How will this phase be project managed?

Acquisition evaluation

Acquisition due diligence is often biased towards internal appraisal. To counter we must ask the following questions:

1.   How inherently attractive are the pharma markets which our target is on (consider its growth drivers and the level of competitive pressure)?

2.   What is our target's underlying competitive position, (for instance, in the strength of its portfolio, the potential of its R&D pipeline) and is it okay, average or weak?

3.   What is the basis of its competitive advantage, and is this likely to be sustainable given anticipated market and competitive change – including potential new drugs being launched by competitors?

4.   How competitive is its cost base (and as against existing players and new entrants and/or distribution channels)?

5.   Are any of its drugs or markets moving into maturity or decline (life-cycle effects) and how long will it be before they came of patent?

6.   What is the strength of its management?

7.   How vulnerable is it likely to be to key staff leaving?

8.   Given our integration plans, how difficult (and uncertain) is integration likely to be?

9.   Where does the business currently make most/least money, and where does it destroy shareholder value (at the present time)?

10.   Where is the business likely to make most/least money in the future?

11.   What can we (genuinely) bring to the party in the way of value-added to the acquisition?

12.   How will this phase be project managed?

Negotiating the deal

The deal is the most important phase of the acquisition project – and one which may be poorly handled by the inexperience. Consider the following:

1.   Do we have a strong and experienced acquisition team – especially in terms of due diligence skills and negotiation skills?

2.   Will the team work well with each other – and avoid getting carried away with the 'thrill of the chase'?

3.   What competition might exist for the deal, and is this likely to push up the price to a level at which we become indifferent as to whether to go ahead or not with the deal?

4.   What is the relative balance in the bargaining power between buyer and seller – what is the relative pressure to buy or sell, and who has the most options?

5.   How skilled is the vendor's team in negotiating – and where are their likely vulnerabilities and weaknesses?

6.   Are we absolutely clear as to what *we are bringing to the party* versus what value is already inherent in the acquisition (so we avoid, in effect, paying twice)?

7.   Are there in-built check-points within the deal-making process for whether we carry on or not?

8.   Who will have the ultimate say over what we are prepared to offer?

Integration

Integration of a pharma company is an activity which will pay off in a very big way, especially as pharma companies tend to have idiosyncratic processes, people, and culture. We must ask the following:

1.   What key synergies are anticipated to be harvested through the acquisition?

2.   What changes are required in order to achieve these synergies – to products, services, operations, systems and processes, structures and people?

3.   Who are the key people who are essential both to protect and develop the business?

4.   How can they be convinced that it is worth backing the organisation following this period of pronounced uncertainty associated with the acquisition, for example through:

- selling the benefits of the acquisition in terms of future opportunity for their own development and reward?
- providing them with a clear role in the change venture?
- spelling out openly the criteria for success and failure?
- protecting their self-respect through active incorporation of 'core best practices' to a new paradigm?
- having a clear and well-communicated strategy for steering change?

5.   Is it planned to announce changes in leadership and structure quickly as opposed to playing a 'wait-and-see' game with the result of mounting uncertainty?

6.   Will changes in systems and control routines be handled with delicacy, sensitivity and sensible timescales set to make changes?

Where systems and control changes are required from 'day one' are there arrangements to support this externally?

7.   How will the issue of 'culture change' be handled, especially where it is intended to integrate a large part of operations? Does this reflect pre-acquisition diagnosis of the key differences in culture between both organisations?

8.   How will learning about the acquisition be secured in terms both of 'what we have got for our money' (both internal and external capability) and also on the effectiveness of integration process?

9.   How will this phase be project managed?

Post review and learning

1.   Given our original strategic objectives were these:

- fully achieved?
- partially achieved?
- not achieved at all?

2.   To what extent were we able to add value to the acquisition, and was this value:

- deliberate? (Or as intended originally.)
- emergent?

3.   How effective was the integration process?

4.   Given 1–3 above, what are the lessons for future acquisitions and for our management of them?

ALLIANCES (JOINT VENTURE) PROJECTS

Whilst pharma acquisitions capture the headlines in the financial press, companies are increasingly moving their corporate strategy forward in a slightly more stealthily fashion through alliances (otherwise known as 'joint ventures'). 'Strategic alliance' can now be defined as:

> *A longer-term strategic partnership between two or more organisations*
> *where there is investment in the venture by all of those partners, sharing*
> *both reward and risk.*

Alliances may be thought of as being *less* risky than acquisitions. It is true that often the *exposure* of an alliance partner may be less (due to sharing of risk and the fact that the commitment, although longer term, is usually not quite so permanent). However, the riskiness of an alliance can be higher due to the following:

- the arrangements are very loose;

- there is a need for a good deal of co-operation and openness;

- alliance partners may often have different aspirations (and possibly ones in tension or conflict), or different levels of bargaining power;

- the strategies of partners may change over time (and alongside that the personal agendas of key players in top management);

- the alliance itself will evolve and change as will its competitive environment.

Some key questions to reflect upon for any pharma alliance (split up into the phases of formation and development) are as follows:

Formation

1. What is the fundamental purpose of the alliance – what distinctive value does it add?

2. Why is it likely to be better than other possible alliances?

3. What are the different options for structuring and resourcing the alliance?

4. To what extent is the alliance well-timed?

5. How are the various needs and competencies of the alliance partners genuinely complementary?

6. To what extent are these needs and competencies in tension or in potential conflict?

7. To what extent is the alliance genuinely (therefore) a 'positive sum game' (or an arrangement where all parties are significantly better off through participating in the alliance)?

8. What is the potential for the alliance leading on into a full acquisition, longer-term?

9. Culturally, are the alliance partners likely to get on with each other: well, satisfactorily or, perhaps, badly?

10. Have all partners got sufficient interest and commitment in the alliance to make it genuinely effective?

11. Will our doing an alliance with another partner(s) only give us a temporary advantage – as it will trigger other alliances in the pharma industry?

12. What are the potential risks and downsides to sustaining our core competencies by depending upon the alliance?

13. Can we learn about how our partners do things really well and apply them elsewhere in our business without our partners becoming antagonistic?

14. How long (realistically) do we think the alliance is likely to last?

15. What does a decision-tree analysis reveal about its expected/ possible pay-offs?

16. Who (if anyone) is likely to become the more dominant partner in the pharma alliance, and if this is not likely to be us, what is the potential value of us being in the alliance?

17. Do any arrangements for potential divorce adequately safeguard our interests?

18. How will the formation of the alliance be project managed?

Development

1. What investment is the alliance likely to require over time, and are alliance partners both able and willing to commit this when the time arrives?

2. What senior management (and other scarce skills) is the alliance likely to need, and who will support this requirement?

3. How will alliance partners conduct any reviews of performance and steer the strategy forward?

4. In the event that the alliance takes off even more successfully than anticipated, how will it cope with this, particularly with regard to:

   - people?
   - structures?
   - financial resources?

5. What processes for change of partners (including new ones coming in, old ones leaving or changes in partner stakes) will be managed?

6. How will alliance development be project managed (for example, what will its key milestones be)?

Checklists for Operational Projects

Besides the more purely 'business development' projects including organic development, acquisitions and alliances, there may also be some major operational projects. These can be grouped (for convenience) under the two main headings of:

- operations expansion;

- cost management and efficiency.

Cost management is becoming increasingly important here, as the pharma industry becomes increasingly competitive.

EXPANSION

1.   Based on organic development projects, what is the potential for relatively easy-to-do expansion?

2.   To what extent can manufacturing capacity be increased:

   - by physical expansion?
   - without physical expansion (and by the 'cunning plan')?
   - by appropriate out-sourcing?
   - by alliance?

3.   What productivity targets (by each and every incremental resource) need to be established?

4.   How will expansion be project managed?

COST MANAGEMENT AND EFFICIENCY

1.   How cost-competitive are we against our existing pharma competitors (now)?

2.   How cost-competitive are we against any new entrants (now)?

3.   How cost competitive are we likely to be (on current plans) vis-à-vis existing competitors and potential entrants?

4.   What are the key cost drivers within our current operational set-up and how can these be (a) incrementally improved and (b) radically challenged (for example with zero-based approaches, that is, working up from a situation of nil resources)?

5.   What are the key value drivers of the business and how can incremental value be added (and harvested) from a lower, or equivalent, or (preferably) a changed cost base?

6.   How can key business processes be re-engineered and simplified to make operations more efficient? (We illustrate the issue of cost management with a substantial case example below).

7.   Which other pharma companies should we benchmark and learn from – either from inside or outside the industry – to become more efficient?

8.   By customer benchmarking are there areas of activity that add little real customer value that we can reduce?

9.   How might cost management and efficiency initiatives be project managed?

CASE EXAMPLE – COST MANAGEMENT PROJECT AT COTSWOLD PHARMACEUTICALS

In this case study we look at how a major pharmacompany looked at its global logistics costs as a project – in order to achieve a major breakthrough. This gives the reader a live illustration of one specific area of the checklists – the last one which we covered on 'Cost Management and Efficiency' checklist.

This is a particularly interesting case, not merely because of the project process but also because of the scale of cost improvements. Pharma companies are understandably sensitive about revealing cost improvements so we are able to reveal more about benefits here by preserving the company's anonymity.

Cotswold Pharmaceuticals is a major company based in the UK with marketing operations worldwide. Over the past ten years it had been transformed from a product-led organisation to one which was market-led, and very strong commercially.

In the 1990s Cotswold faced pressures to improve its financial performance – following Board-level changes. The logistics function accounted for a considerable amount of Cotswold's costs (and its value added), particularly as Cotswold's sales were world-wide. These costs were also relatively high because of the sophisticated nature of the product, which was concerned with cancer-related therapies.

The Problem – and Opportunity

Initially the 'problem' of driving logistics costs down was framed as simply that – cost reduction. But rapidly it was realised that costs couldn't just be managed downwards like that without unpleasant side effects (for instance, lost customers or rise in costs elsewhere).

The Head of Cotswold's Global Logistics function, who we will call Ray Scott, decided to shift discussion above the project's scope and objectives.

'How can we make major reductions in Cotswold's logistics costs?

To:

'How can we manage logistics costs for both financial and competitive advantage?'

This change in emphasis within the project scope had a number of key implications:

- besides cost reduction, Cotswold would also be seeking opportunities for extra revenue generation;
- any cost-cutting measures would be carefully probed to establish whether they might erode Cotswold's competitive position;
- any changes in 'how we do things around here' in logistics needed to be managed in unison with changes (and their projects) in other business processes, particularly in manufacturing, marketing and information systems.

The review of costs was not purely inward-facing and was supplemented by competitive benchmarking – to establish whether Cotswold really did have 'a problem' and also to target continuous improvement.

Instead of leaping into project planning prematurely, Cotswold's management decided to conduct a thorough project diagnosis, and only then to formulate a project strategy.'

The early process – diagnosis and data collection

Ray Scott orchestrated a two-day workshop in logistics which was preceded by a one-day workshop on manufacturing. Participants in the logistics workshops were drawn from different parts of Cotswold's overseas operations world-wide making it a multi-regional and multi-functional project. This proved invaluable not merely in obtaining data but also in building a commitment to effect change.

The workshop was attended by between 12 and 15 managers (different staff attending at different times). Ray Scott used one of us as facilitator.

Managing the outputs

The sheer amount of ideas for scoping the project generated by syndicate groups on that first day came as a surprise to everyone. The range of opportunities generated itself became a problem for the process.

By continually sorting out the emerging ideas into a set of issue groups, it proved possible to generate a full issue framework. By using a facilitator there was always someone with their 'hands and brain free' to collect and structure issues and options.

The AID grid (see Chapter 4) enabled the issues (and opportunities) to be broken down into a number of natural areas. (Incidentally, this grid was invented during the workshop itself.) First, we distinguished between areas of costs which were variable and shorter-term offering relatively quick opportunities for saving. Second, there were areas of cost which might have been regarded as 'fixed' but in the longer-term were variable. Thirdly, there was a big issue about service responsiveness and ensuring that customers were neither over-or under-serviced. Finally, there was a need for clear objectives and performance measures to be set, particularly using competitive benchmarking.

The initial workshop only served to get the ball rolling. Key imperatives were:

- the need to collect some (often basic) cost data and analyse these in new ways;
- the process of winning approval for organisational and operational change and change in how customer needs are dealt with;
- the need to focus on a small number of cost breakthrough project areas and deliver results over a period often extending over two to three years;
- the role of external benchmarking in targeting improvement, generating ideas to reconfigure processes, and as an ongoing check on performance during project implementation;
- the imperative to change performance measures and feedback processes to make the project more balanced, and cross-functional,

The definition of the 'project result' and its value was far from self-evident, rather than easy to put numbers on. For example, one of the particularly interesting outputs was service responsiveness. First, there were areas where Cotswold was making shipments to customers more frequently than they actually needed. Second, there were instances where customers sought 'urgent deliveries'. Cotswold responded by delivering a separate shipment without any premium price for delivery. By putting a 'tax' on special deliveries, almost as if by magic, their very need disappeared as customers and company sought to anticipate requirements sooner. This again illustrates the need to have a 'cunning' plan (or innovative plan).

Net cost reductions (or revenue increases) per annum of *over 15 per cent of logistics costs* were targeted as a result of this exercise (as a 'gap' analysis). Over 70 options/areas of opportunity were identified which were then prioritised using AID analysis. A sub-set of these were translated into detailed action plans and implemented over the next two to three years. This highlights the need to filter and refine the 'things to do' (or the total work-breakdown analysis) into some deliverable packages of work which will each leverage value over cost and effort.

As one measure of success, we see that the cost management breakthrough project at Cotswold Technology exceeded its original expectations.

> 'When we started out we were running at something in the order of (distribution costs), a percentage of sales just over 10 per cent. We are now at 8 per cent.'

Savings in distribution costs subsequently represent about 15 per cent of Cotswold's annual profits two years later, highlighting the significance of the cost management project just in one key business function alone. This cost reduction has contributed significantly to the quadrupling of Cotswold's share price over a four-year period.

But implementing breakthrough cost management projects effectively is not easy. It is time-consuming to gain full involvement of key stakeholders at a variety of levels through the diagnosis, planning and implementation phases (see again Chapter 4). Ray Scott reflects on the implementation hurdles for such projects.

> 'The honest truth is that we under-estimated (the amount of work required in implementation). This was double at least what we expected...you (need to) agree with your (internal) customers what is important and, in our case, the customer is the commercial people making it a multi-regional and multi-functional project.'

The project's difficulty over time curve was far greater than was originally anticpated. This reflects the need to remember that any project which is technically, economically and politically complex in the pharma industry can take 50 per cent longer than anticipated. When you have not done a similar project before, it can easily take twice as long. One of the ways of mitigating the effect of this misplaced over-optimism is to benchmark how similar projects have been managed successfully in other organisations.

Lessons

There are a number of very specific lessons from our discussion of the cost management project at Cotswold Pharmaceuticals. These are:

- How the original problem (which the project is aimed at) is framed is of vital importance to achieving its goal.
- Sufficient time must be created for both workshop preparation and for issue generation, diagnosis and evaluation of project diagnosis and strategy.
- Although diagnosis frequently yields a very large number of opportunities which then have to be skilfully evaluated and prioritised, using the 'AID' grid.
- Some large opportunities may be longer term or may be perceived to be relatively difficult. However, these do not tend to go away but need to be brought back on to the agenda.
- It is crucial to get the right people involved at the diagnosis stage of the project – from a variety of functions – so that they own the need for change and for continuing improvement.
- There is invariably a good deal of organisational politics associated with making the project management process work. This needs to be tackled directly, otherwise much of the potential gains will be harvested.
- To sustain the benefits, key performance measures need to be defined for the project and also made more externally orientated, for instance by competitive benchmarking.
- There is invariably more work than the managers anticipate in the detailed planning and implementation process for a project of this nature – some of the areas for greatest financial benefit do not get addressed because of perceived implementation difficulty.

The increasingly competitive pressure we have seen over the past decade in the pharma industry has put the spotlight very much on costs. Sometimes this spotlight has been focused purely internally and without regard for the interdependencies within the business value system. Cost management projects are likely to become increasingly important within the pharma industry and need to be skilfully and professionally managed in order to achieve real business benefits – and to avoid destroying shareholder value inadvertently.

Note

For a decision tree of where to start in the pharma project management process please refer to Figures 8.1, 8.2 and 8.3. For a review of how the key tools interrelate with one another, see Figure 8.4. This highlights the key linkage between the techniques covered in this book. Finally, when managing a pharma project the issue often arises as to how easy it might be for others to imitate one's innovative strategic ideas. Do use these checklists for all pharma projects which you will be undertaking in the future.

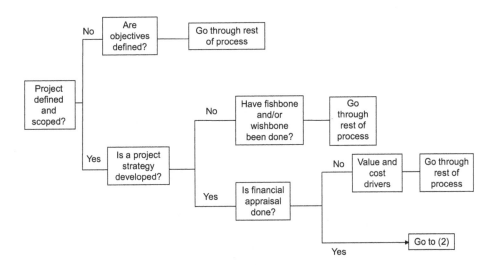

Figure 8.1   Decision tree (1) of (3)

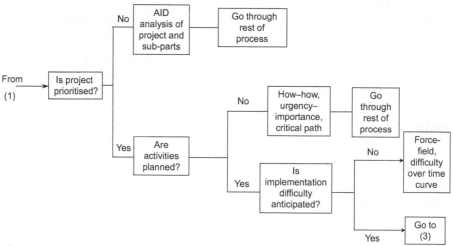

Figure 8.2   Decision tree (2) of (3)

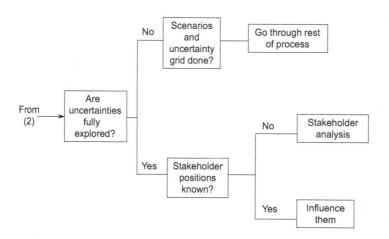

Figure 8.3   Decision tree (3) of (3)

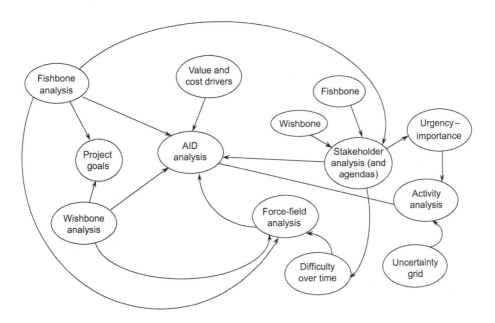

Figure 8.4   **Interdependencies: Implementation and project management tools**

9

Conclusion

Summary of Key Lessons

In this short concluding chapter we give you an overview of the key lessons of this book and suggest some next steps for you to implement.

We began by looking at how project management can be used to achieve major breakthroughs in the pharma industry, not merely of drug development but also through other areas such as business development, change and technology, infrastructure and people development. We saw that conventional project management, which has been brought in from more traditional industries, is not really fully up for the job.

In some ways the case of personal computers and project management software packages has exacerbated this problem – by over-focusing on very detailed and highly determinate project plans – which are often rigid and unrealistic.

One of the most critical additions to pharma project management is that of strategic thinking. Strategic thinking helps pharma project managers by helping understand their project's external and internal environment more thoroughly, and also through its emphasis on options, not only for *what* projects you do, but also on *how* you do them. In addition, our focus on strategy as the 'cunning plan' helps to provide innovative thinking about project positioning, processes and getting the maximum out of scarce resources in the least time.

We then went on to illustrate how strategic thinking helped one of the us to manage a whole variety of projects at ICI Biosciences, also reducing organisational and personal stress. We then looked at the pharma project process, which emphasised diagnosis, strategy and learning as being equally important phases alongside the traditional ones of project planning and implementation.

In Chapter 2 we took a closer look at the links between pharma projects and pharma business strategy. Here we saw the impact of external changes in the industry putting increasing pressure on costs and on timelines. In addition we saw that mergers in the industry have also created the need for structure and culture change projects. Increased competition has also meant more focus on cost management costs. Even drug development projects are now increasingly difficult and onerous through increased regulatory requirements.

Instead of recognising these realities and becoming more focused and strategic in its approach to project management, the pharma industry has typically responded by trying to squeeze even more out of less. Conventional project management techniques have often been deployed as methodologies to put even more pressure on professionals within the industry, causing project slippages and staff burn-out.

This phenomenon, which the authors have witnessed across a variety of pharma companies, is frequently counter-productive. We first looked at how projects can actually play a more constructive role in implementing business strategy in the pharma industry. We introduced the idea of the 'strategy mix' through 'deliberate', 'emergent', 'detergent' and 'submergent' strategies. These categories can manifest themselves both *within* the business strategy itself, and also at the project level.

These forms of strategy are helpful in recognising when a project is, or might be about to go off course, and needs to be brought back into a 'deliberate strategy' mode. The strategy mix is also helpful when a project manager is tasked with understanding the project's strategic objectives; frequently these are hard to establish where there is a very fluid strategy ('emergent', 'submergent' or 'emergency'), and thus the links to the business strategy are unclear.

Here the pharma project manager needs to make assumptions about what the strategy is supposed to be, and to seek greater clarity by upward management. (Essential thoughts here are: 'These are my strategic assumptions about the role of the project – am I right in my suppositions?')

Having examined how strategies and projects tend to develop in an incremental and often haphazard manner, we then proposed the pharma project management process as a way of minimising the impact of frequently imperfect decision-making (top-down) within pharma companies. This is done by elaborating how project programmes help to manage interdependencies between projects.

In Chapter 3 we went through scoping the pharma project, defining and the diagnosing its key issues and also identifying its key stakeholders and its likely difficulty – in advance. The issue of to source activities in or out possibly with the help of the CRO was then explored. To achieve this, we went through a number of techniques which are not to be found in traditional project management – the industry's current main model.

We found that fishbone and wishbone and from-to analysis were frequently helpful for scoping a project and defining its objectives. Also gap analysis helped towards setting stretching but achievable objectives. Performance drivers also helped us anchor the project's rationale in shifts in performance – particularly pharma projects not directly involving drug development.

In Chapter 4 we then examined how a project strategy and more detailed plans could be developed. This entailed using the project option grid to evaluate and prioritise different projects, and also different ways of implementing them.

Once a project has now been more clearly identified we were able to do more micro-level prioritisation of the key elements in the how-how or work breakdown structure analysis that were needed to achieve the project's result. Only at this point did we pick up the more traditional analysis techniques of work breakdown analysis, critical path analysis and Gantt charts which are so much the focus currently within the industry. As one pharma professional reflected after coming on the authors' workshop:

> *Before the workshop I was quite good at planning microscopically when the clinical research project would be finished by – although I was often way out with my estimates. Now I am far more concerned about doing the right project in the first place, doing it in the best (and in a most 'cunning way') and continually adapting my plans as the project environment changes. I am also thinking a lot more about the stakeholders and now realise that these 'softer' aspects of project management are vital to running a successful project. Indeed, these issues are probably more important than focussing primarily on producing elaborate Gantt charts.*

In addition to those more traditional techniques (many of which can be managed by project management software, which we discussed), we have also incorporated the very powerful techniques of force-field analysis and stakeholder analysis into the process. These techniques (now being adopted in many other industries to enrich traditional project management) are a great help in predicting timelines and also in obtaining the necessary resources on a just-in-time basis, to prevent delay.

Finally we examined the need to map out the projects' most critical interdependencies, and to anticipate how (and by whom) these should be managed. This once again emphasised the importance of understanding the project's environment – and strategic thinking.

In Chapter 5 we then took a look at pharma project evaluation, beginning with the business value system, which was defined as the system of aligned activities to which a pharma project adds value. We explored the processes of financial evaluation – in the pharma industry context – and then looked at how uncertainty and scenario analysis could be used to get a better understanding of project value and cost drivers. We also looked at financial evaluation, focusing in on a drug development example.

In Chapter 6 we examined the imperatives of project mobilisation, control and learning and also how project dynamics could be anticipated and tracked. In Chapter 7 we were able to explore the need to influence people and behaviours, and how these behaviours could be more proactively managed. We also touched on the various team roles which made up a more effective project team.

In Chapter 8 we took you through some more detailed project checklists, first dealing with organic business development projects (including drug development), and we then went on to consider acquisitions, alliances and organisational change projects. Finally we went through a case study of a pharma cost breakthrough project, which delivered major benefits over a two-year period.

Implementation and Next Steps

We now make the following suggestions for implementation and next steps:

- whenever starting a project, re-read Chapter 3 on 'Defining Pharmaceutical Projects';

- when doing conventional project planning, also use techniques like force-field analysis and the difficulty over time curve, and the uncertainty grid to get a reality-check on feasibility of timelines;

- use stakeholder analysis at *each and every stage of the project*;

- think about the personality types and roles within your team (for example through Belbin, Chapter 7);

- use the checklists in Chapter 8 whenever starting a project which you are less familiar with;

- adapt the figures and various tables within your own process;

- do not take on any project which is clearly not particularly attractive (to the business) and is particularly difficult (the AID analysis).

From an organisational point of view it is important to remember that improving and adapting project management processes within the pharma industry requires a well thought-out intervention strategy. It is not really enough just to send a few, isolated individuals on a public project management course. In addition, the following are needed:

- The tailoring and official adoption of a more comprehensive set of tools for managing pharma products than is conventionally found within the industry.

- Training for 'intact teams' in tailored project management methodologies; this can involve their work on cases from other companies and/or work on their own issues. This can be typically accomplished in around 2–3 days.

- This training needs then to be supported – either by internal facilitation or perhaps by an external helpline – for a number of months. This period then allows start to pilot the process on real issues. Further reinforcement should occur through a review workshop – focusing on what has been learnt through early application.

- The process (and particularly the evaluation/portfolio management techniques) need to be formally adopted by top management and actually used for their own issues.

Finally, so that you don't forget these lessons from our book, it is good to bear in mind the following story:

> *Once upon a time an enterprising turkey gathered the flock together and, with demonstrations and instructions, taught them how to fly. All afternoon they enjoyed soaring, reaching new vistas. After the training was over, all the turkeys walked home.*
>
> *(Anon.)*

Moral: Don't slip back into turkey (project) management.

Good luck with your endeavours!

Laura Brown and Tony Grundy, 2011.

For further information...

There are a few training companies running public training courses on pharma project management. The authors would recommend Management Forum (www.management-forum.co.uk) who specialise in providing courses for the pharma industry. If you are interested in-company courses which can be tailored for your specific needs, please contact the authors (lbrown@ntlworld.com). Laura is contactable on lbrown@ntlworld.com and Tony on tony.grundy1@virginmedia.com – should you have any queries on the process, or desire to know even more about how it can be tailored to your company and/or your staff trained in it. A help-line (via e-mail lbrown@ntlworld.com) is available if you would like any assistance with the tools and techniques covered in this book.

Glossary of Key Project Management Definitions

Activity
: A discrete area of action which leads towards project goals. An activity normally has an expected duration, an expected cost, and expected resource requirement. Activities are often subdivided into tasks.

Control
: The process of comparing actual performance with planned performance, analysing variances, evaluating possible alternatives, and taking appropriate corrective action as needed.

Cost
: The direct and indirect cost of achieving the project result.

Critical activity
: Any activity on a critical path. Most commonly determined by using critical path analysis method.

Critical path
: That path through the network activities of a project which will determine the time to complete the project. The critical path will generally change from time to time as activities are completed ahead of or behind schedule.

Critical path analysis	A network analysis technique used to predict project duration by analysing which sequence of activities (path) has the least amount of scheduling flexibility (the least amount of float).
Deliverables	The specific benefits of a project (or phase of a project). In particular, any measurable, tangible, verifiable outcome, result, or item that must be produced to complete the project or part of the project.
Float	That time planned into the project or project stage/phase which allows for possible over run elsewhere.
Gantt chart	A graphic bar chart display of schedule-related information. In a typical Gantt chart, activities or other project elements are listed down the left side of the chart, dates are shown across the top, and activity durations are shown as date-placed horizontal bars.
Milestones	The time by which a particular deliverable has to be achieved.
Network	The interdependent activities which all have to be completed – and in a particular sequence to deliver the project's result.
Objectives	The overarching goals of the project (more general than specific deliverables).
Plan	The detailed programme of activities which will deliver the project on time.
Programme	A group of related projects managed in a coordinated way.

Project	A complex set of activities which have the intention to deliver a specific result at a pre-targeted time and cost. Projects are temporary endeavours undertaken to create a unique product or service.
Project life-cycle	A collection of generally sequential project stages/phases whose name and number are determined by the control needs of the organisation or organisations involved in the project.
Project network diagram	Any schematic display of the logical relationships of project activities. Always drawn from left to right to reflect prject chronology. Often incorrectly referred as a PERT (performance evaluation and review technique) chart.
Project schedule	The planned dates for performing activities and the planned dates for meeting milestones.
Result	The collective deliverables of the project (both in terms of quantity and quality).
Scope	The size, duration and scale of impact of a project.
Stakeholder	Those individuals (or groups of individuals) who might either (a) give the project a 'go-ahead' (b) be influential on that decision (c) implement/manage the project (d) be affected (e) be affected by it otherwise (as users of even as 'victims').
Strategy	The 'cunning' plan which will guide the project to a successful conclusion – and with competitive advantage.

Time	The total duration not merely to complete the project activities but also realise its deliverables.
Work breakdown structure (WBS) or how–how analysis	A deliverable-orientated grouping of project elements which organises and defines the total scope of the project. Each descending level represents an increasingly detailed definition of a project component.

Bibliography

Ansoff, H.I., *Corporate Strategy*, McGraw-Hill, New York, 1965.

Braybrook, D. and Lindblom, E., *A Strategy of Decision*, Free Press, New York, 1963.

Goldratt, E.M., *Theory of Constraints*, North River Press, Massachusetts, 1990.

Grundy, A.N., *Strategic Behaviour*, FT Pitman Publishing, London, 1987.

Grundy A.N., *Corporate Strategy and Financial Decisions*, Kogan Page, London, 1992.

Grundy, A.N., *Implementing Strategic Change*, Kogan Page, London, 1993a.

Grundy, A.N., *Strategic Learning*, McGraw Hill, London, 1993b.

Grundy, A.N., *Breakthrough Strategies for Growth*, FT Pitman Publishing, London, 1995.

Grundy, A.N., *Exploring Strategic Financial Management*, Prentice Hall, Hemel Hempsted, 1998a.

Grundy, A.N., *Harnessing Strategic Behaviour*, Financial Times Publishing, London, 1998b.

Grundy, A.N., 'Strategic Project Management and Strategic Behaviour', *International Journal of Project Management*, Vol. 18, pp. 93–103, 2000.

Johnson, G. and Scholes, K., *Exploring Corporate Strategy*, Prentice Hall, Hemel Hempsted, 1992.

Lewin, K., *A Dynamic Theory of Personality*, McGraw Book Company, New York, 1935.

March, J.E. and Simon, H.A., *Organizations*, John Wiley, New York, 1958.

Mintzberg, H., *The Rise and Fall of Strategic Planning*, Prentice Hall, Hemel Hempsted, 1994.

Mitroff, I. and Linstone, H.A., *The Unbounded Mind*, Oxford University Press, Oxford, 1993.

Peters, T. and Waterman, R.H., *Organizations*, John Wiley, New York, 1982.

Piercey, N.P., 'Diagnosing and Solving Implementation Problems in Strategic Planning', *Journal of General Management*, Vol. 15, no.1, pp. 19–38, 1989.

Porter, E.M., *Competitive Strategy*, The Free Press, Macmillan, New York, 1980.

Porter, E.M., *Competitive Advantage,* The Free Press, Macmillan, New York, 1985.

Quinn, J.B., *Strategies for Change: Logical Incrementalism*, Homewood, Irwin, 1980.

Stalk, E., *Competing Against Time*, The Free Press, New York, 1990.

Sun Tzu, *The Art of War*, Shambhala, London and Boston, 1991.

Verny A. and Kingmann I., 'A 6 Month Process for Planning Multi-centre Clinical Trials', *Applied Clinical Trials*, pp. 58–61, February 2003.

Vogel, R. and Schober, N. 'Evaluating Proposals from CROs', *Good Clinical Practice*, SCRIP Reports, BS 862, pp. 111–112, 1997.

Vogel, R. and Schober, N. 'Achieving Results with CROs: Requesting and Evaluating Proposals from CROs'. *Applied Clinical Trials,* Vol. 2, no. 12, pp. 32–41.

Index

About the Authors

Dr Laura Brown, BSc, PhD, MBA, Diploma in Clinical Science, is Director of Laura Brown Training and Development. She is also Director of the MSc programme in Clinical Research, School of Pharmacy at the University of Cardiff and Director of The Organisation for Professionals in Regulatory Affairs' (TOPRA) MSc in Regulatory Affairs. Laura regularly presents pharmaceutical public project management courses through Management Forum Ltd (www.management-forum.co.uk), and is available for in-company workshops and courses.

Laura has 20 years' experience of the Pharmaceuticals Industry and has worked with GSK, Hoechst Marion Roussel, Good Clinical Research Practices and MDS. She has worked as a Life Cycle Project Manager, Clinical Research Manager and as Head of Training for a pharmaceutical training company.

Her particular specialisms are: pharmaceutical project management, regulatory change and pharma management skills. She has facilitated strategy development in the pharmaceutical industry.

Laura is co-author of five books on management and is author of the latest *SCRIP* report in GCP (Good Clinical Practice).

Dr Laura Brown can be contacted at:

Laura Brown Training and Development
126 Rickmansworth Lane
Chalfont St Peter
Bucks SL9 0RQ
England

+44 (0) 1494 873566
laura.brown.training@googlemail.com
www.laurabrowndevelopment.com

Dr Tony Grundy, MA, MBA, MSc, MPhil, FCA and PhD is Director of Cambridge Corporate Development and Visiting Lecturer at Henley Business School. He is also Academic Advisor on TOPRA's MSc in Regulatory Affairs.

Tony has researched the strategic and financial appraisal of major projects, and the strategic behaviour of teams involved in complex projects. Tony specialises in strategic thinking, strategic team working and project appraisal in a variety of contexts, and has also consulted extensively in the pharmaceutical industry.

Tony is co-author of 17 books.

Dr Tony Grundy can be contacted at: tony.grundy1@virginmedia.com or on +44 (0) 7710 198462.

www.tonygrundy.com